SIDE KICK

Achieving Kicking Excellence™

Shawn Kovacich

Printed in the United States of America

Library of Congress Card Number: 2004090167

ISBN #0-9707496-9-4

Table of Contents

Disclaimer

Please note that the author and/or publisher of this instructional book are **Not Responsible** in any manner whatsoever, for any injury, which may occur by reading and/or following the instructions located within this book. The techniques described within this book are sophisticated in nature and have the potential to cause serious damage to the reader or readers, if performed incorrectly. Therefore, it is essential that the reader or readers of this book consult a qualified and competent physician before following any of the activities, physical or otherwise, which are described within this book. This book is intended to be used as a supplemental training aid, and should be used as such, under the guidance of a qualified and competent martial arts instructor.

Copyrights & Trademarks

Acknowledgements

I would like to take this opportunity to dedicate this book to the following athletes who have had a profound impact on me as a person, and as a martial artist.

George Foreman, World Heavyweight Boxing Champion

Julie Moss, Ironman triatholon athlete

Evel Knievel, World's Greatest Daredevil

This book would never have been published without the assistance of the following people who have contributed their time, energy, and skill in the creation of this book.

Doug and Cassie Bender for the use of their facility used in principle photography.

The staff and owners of Sports West Gym for the use of their facility and equipment used in principle photography.

Jessica Bronder for her assistance, and Ron Dunlap for his participation in this book.

"Before I studied the art, a punch to me was just a punch, a kick was just a kick. After I studied the art, a punch was no longer a punch, a kick was no longer a kick. Now that I understand the art, a punch is just a punch, a kick is just a kick." —Bruce Lee

About the Author

Watching Shawn Kovacich teach is like watching a college professor explaining quantum physics in such a way, that it is as easily understandable as a current episode of Sesame Street. With his unique ability to analyze and break down any kick to its most basic level, he then explains in exacting detail, the important aspects of each and every component in the kick. This gives the student a complete and detailed analysis of every movement in the kick from beginning to end.

Mr. Kovacich started his martial arts training at the age of seventeen, and took to it like the proverbial duck to water, earning his first-degree black belt after two years and nine months of training. His teaching ability became evident early on in his training and he often assisted his instructors with newer students.

The most influential moment of Mr. Kovacich's early martial arts training came when he was privileged to not only witness, but also to participate in two of his instructors, Shihan Brian Knechtges and Sensei Ben Hunn's, third degree black belt test, in which Shihan Knechtges and Sensei Hunn had to fight continuously for 100 minutes each against a fresh opponent every minute. Punches and kicks were not pulled and the two men were pushed beyond all normal standards of human endurance. Both men not only prevailed and were awarded their third degree black belts, but they also became a source of inspiration for Mr. Kovacich. Years later, he would take this test not once, but twice, and emerged triumphant both times.

Shortly after testing for and receiving his first-degree black belt, Mr. Kovacich accomplished another prestigious goal while participating in a charity fund-raiser. That goal, which he easily reached, was the first of what was to become two world records for endurance high kicking certified by The Guinness Book of World Records.

Mr. Kovacich has been an active instructor, teaching in as many as three schools at a time since 1985. He has taught students of all ages from six to sixty-eight, and from all walks of life, including law enforcement personnel, military personnel, correctional officers, mental health professionals, etc. Since the early 90's, he has also been an active competitor in bare knuckle full-contact karate. Competing in such prestigious tournaments throughout the United States such as the Sabaki Challenge, the Great Northwest Sabaki Satellite, the U.S. Shidokan Open, and the Shidokan Team USA. Mr. Kovacich still actively competes in these tournaments as well as being one of the top Instructor/Coaches for the former USTU (United States Tae Kwon Do Union) national and international tae kwon do competitions.

Mr. Kovacich is currently a fourth-degree black belt in both Karate and Tae Kwon Do. Powerful and intelligent, he is constantly analyzing every movement in a kick in order to get the most speed and power available. He is one of only a handful of instructors who can improve anyone's kicking ability regardless of their physical ability or non-ability, or their martial arts style. Unyielding power is what makes Shawn Kovacich a world-class fighter, but what makes him truly unique is his analytical and innovative teaching ability.

Preface

In an unarmed self-defense encounter, your kicking skills or lack thereof, can be the deciding factor between victory and defeat. I can still remember back in my high school days when kicking was considered dirty fighting, and seldom if ever used. Things certainly have changed since the late 70's and early 80's. Today kicking is not only used more frequently, but it also ranks as perhaps the most versatile and underrated weapon that you have in your personal arsenal. With the noted exception of your head, and I don't mean as a physical weapon, but in your ability to intelligently avoid the threat, and if you are unable to avoid it, to overcome it as quickly and efficiently as possible.

Presented here are several different reasons why you should learn and practice the kicking skills presented not only in this book, but also from a certified and competent martial arts instructor.

1. The majority of people do not know how to kick, and therefore tend to rely mainly on their hands, giving them only two weapons. By learning how to kick, you have doubled your available weapons from two (your hands) to four (your hands and feet).
2. Your legs are the most powerful physical weapons that you have in your arsenal. They are several times stronger than your arms and have a greater reach.
3. Kicking can be your "Ace in the Hole" when fighting. Used properly, your opponent will not expect it and will never know what hit him.
4. Kicking adds another dimension to your fighting abilities by allowing you to kick at the same time your hands are defending, attacking, or grabbing your opponent.
5. If you wind up on the ground, kicking can give you that extra split second in order to keep your opponent at bay while you regain your standing position. And finally,
6. Kicking helps keep you in shape by constantly strengthening and stretching the legs and lower torso. It is all too easy to forget that your legs are carrying you around everyday. Without them where would you be?

The exact reason why you have decided to begin utilizing the kicking skills taught in this book depends upon your own personal needs and interests. You may enjoy it because of the stress reduction and physical fitness benefits, or simply because you enjoy the physical challenge that kicking correctly presents. While others enjoy the sporting, or competition aspects of the tournament arena. However, for most people, their primary reason for practicing these kicking skills is for self-defense.

Irregardless of the reason, the materials presented in this book are beneficial to anyone who wants to improve their kicking ability, whether it is the martial artist, tournament competitor, aerobic kickboxing enthusiast, or the self-defense advocate.

While this book and the material presented within it are invaluable to the individual who does not have the opportunity to learn in a formal setting, it is also a tremendous benefit to those who are fortunate enough to have access to a qualified and competent instructor. A privilege and an honor one should never take for granted.

It is my hope that every person who picks up this book and studies it, walks away with an in-depth understanding of how to correctly perform all of the intricate aspects of the Back Leg Side Kick and its 10 most common variations. As the individual becomes increasingly proficient at performing their kicking and fighting skills, their need to exercise self-discipline, self-control, and responsibility increases dramatically.

What exactly is a Side Kick?

I am often asked this question and the best response that I have come up with is simply this, "A properly executed Side Kick performed by a man (or woman), can be likened to a pool cue striking a cue ball on a pool table."

Note:

All of the kicks shown in this book were executed with the right leg. Therefore, in order to execute these kicks with the left leg, simply switch each kicks description from left to right and vice versa where appropriate. I have included a complete description of Step-Behind Side Kick utilizing the left leg at the end of the Back Leg Side Kick Variations chapter. Use this as a guideline for switching the description of the other kicks for use with the left leg.

How To Use This Book

Although you can learn all of the techniques shown in this book on your own, there are many different subtleties and variables present within each of the kicks shown that true mastery of any of these kicks can only be gained under the knowledgeable eye of a qualified and competent instructor. This book is designed to be a reference manual for the instructor, and a textbook for the student. In order to learn from this book, you must first grasp a basic understanding on how to learn. In explaining this, I like to use the story of learning how to walk.

Every one of us, you included, came into this world as a baby. Did you run marathons as a baby? Of course not. You weren't even able to do anything for yourself, except for maybe making messes. And everybody has been through that, no matter whom or what they are, we all started out as babies. Now how does a baby first get around? Does he walk or run? No of course not, a baby first gets around by being carried. Then as the baby's muscles get stronger and he gets a little older he starts to crawl. And in no time at all, he gets pretty good at it and watch out. He is all over the place in no time at all and seemingly faster than greased lightning. After awhile crawling gets kind of old and he begins to start learning how to walk. Mom and Dad are their holding his hand as he staggers across the room like a drunken sailor on a Saturday night.

Of course there are the falls and spills that happen as he tries walking on his own, but such is the process of learning. After a while he starts walking on his own and then comes the baby run, which if you are a parent or have ever baby sat a small child you know exactly what I am talking about. It begins with you looking away for just a second and then bang, he's off like a thoroughbred at the Kentucky Derby going for the Triple Crown, and almost as fast. Eventually the baby grows into a child and learns how to run and jump and do all kinds of things.

Of course none of these would have been possible if he hadn't first been carried, then taught to crawl, and had his hand held as he learned to walk, and perhaps just as important, received all those bumps and bruises from falling down and getting back up and trying it again.

The key to learning from this book is to be patient, start slow and take it in steps. Don't skip steps or rush the learning process. Years went into the making of this book in order to give you the best possible source of information on how to correctly execute the kicks presented within.

Go to the Doctor:
You should always consult with a qualified and competent physician before trying any of the techniques described in this book.

Read:
Take this book and read it cover to cover several times, before attempting to execute any of the techniques presented in this book.

Study and Learn:
Learn the who, what, where, when, why, and how's of the anatomy and principles behind the kicks presented in this book. Remember that ignorance may be

bliss, but knowledge truly is power.

Warm-up and Stretching:

Always warm-up and stretch thoroughly and properly before participating in any physical activity. An ounce of prevention is worth a pound of cure.

Take One Step at a Time:

When writing this book, I designed it so that each kick was broken down into several different sections with several technical points in each section. All of this was done so that you could full understand how to correctly execute each of the 11 kicks presented. With the understanding that once you had learned all of the technical points in each section, that you would then put them all together until you were able to perform each movement in every section of the kick as one continuous movement.

Let's use the primary kick Back Leg Side Kick as an example, now the best way to understand this is to look at it on a mathematical level. By this I mean that you are going to learn this kick on a $1 + 1 = 2$ level. Each number one is representative of a technical point that is included in each section. For example Fighting Position has seven technical points. Here is what I mean.

1. Position of your feet = 1
2. Position of your knees = 1
3. Position of your upper body = 1
4. Position of your hands and elbows = 1
5. Position of your back = 1
6. Position of your head = 1
7. Position of your eyes = 1

For a total of 7 technical points.

Now when you look at all of the technical points in each section of a Back Leg Side Kick, it would look like this.

Fighting Position = $1 + 1 + 1 + 1 + 1 + 1 + 1 = 7$
Raise Knee = $1 + 1 + 1 + 1 + 1 + 1 + 1 + 1 = 8$
Coil = $1 + 1 + 1 + 1 + 1 + 1 + 1 + 1 = 8$
Midway to Impact = $1 + 1 + 1 + 1 + 1 + 1 + 1 + 1 = 8$
Impact = $1 + 1 + 1 + 1 + 1 + 1 + 1 + 1 = 8$
Recoil = $1 + 1 + 1 + 1 + 1 + 1 + 1 + 1 = 8$
Lower Knee = $1 + 1 + 1 + 1 + 1 + 1 + 1 + 1 = 8$
Return to Fighting Position = $1 + 1 + 1 + 1 + 1 + 1 + 1 = 7$

For a total of 62 technical points.

What this book was designed to do was to have you fully practice each section until each of the technical points in each section becomes second nature to you. Then you will go onto the next section and do the same thing until you have learned each of the technical points in each section. After that has been accomplished, you will then put each of the sections together one at a time until you are able to perform the entire sequence of movements correctly. For example:

1. Fighting Position
2. Fighting Position + Raise Knee

3. Fighting Position + Raise Knee + Coil
4. Fighting Position + Raise Knee + Coil + Midway to Impact
5. Fighting Position + Raise Knee + Coil + Midway to Impact + Impact
6. Fighting Position + Raise Knee + Coil + Midway to Impact + Impact + Recoil
7. Fighting Position + Raise Knee + Coil + Midway to Impact + Impact + Recoil + Lower Knee
8. Fighting Position + Raise Knee + Coil + Midway to Impact + Impact + Recoil + Lower Knee + Return to Fighting Position

Ideally, you should execute any kick without conscious thought and in one single fluid motion. The execution of the kick should be instinctive in nature, rather than an action or reaction, which in both cases are infinitely slower than acting instinctively. However, just like a baby, you must first go through the entire learning process until executing the kick becomes as natural and without thought as breathing.

Learn the Primary Kick First:

This is pretty much self-explanatory, since everything else is based on the Back Leg Side Kick. Once you learn this primary kick, all of the other variations will be much easier to learn and execute.

Practice, Practice, Practice:

I have heard it said that one must practice any given technique 1,000 times before they know it. I totally and completely disagree. You should correctly practice any technique 3,000 to 5,000 times to learn it, 10,000 times correctly to know it, and a lifetime of practice to master it.

Read this book regularly:

Use this book as a reference guide on a regular basis. As a general rule-of-thumb, every time you practice a Side Kick 1,000 times you should have read this book at least once.

Quality Supervision:

Whenever possible, you should always practice under the watchful eye of a qualified and competent martial arts instructor.

Basic Anatomy of the Side Kick

In this chapter, I will attempt to give you a basic understanding of the primary muscular groups and bones in the skeletal system that form the anatomical basis of a Side Kick. I will do this by listing each of the muscle and bones separately and then at the end of each description, I will provide an explanation as to their role in the correct execution of a Back Leg Side Kick. Although the entire body is utilized in the correct execution of a Side Kick, I will only be concentrating on the muscle and skeletal structure of the lower back, hips, legs, and feet.

BONES:

The skeleton of the leg is composed of the femur (thigh bone), tibia and fibula (calf bones), and the patella (kneecap). These bones have three primary sites of articulation; the hip joint, formed by the head of the femur and the acetabulum of the pelvis, the knee joint, formed by the joining of the lower end of the femur, the patella, and the superior end of the tibia and fibula, and the ankle, formed by the articulation between the tibia and the tarsus. The legs are responsible for bearing a great deal of weight and are subjected to intense vertical and lateral stresses, especially at the knee joint. Consequently, the bones of the leg are often cracked or broken, and the knee, hip and ankle joint are particularly susceptible to fracture, strain, sprain, and dislocation.

Each foot is made up of twenty-six bones, which form the ankle, top and bottom of the foot, and toes. These bones are articularly specialized, allowing a wide range of flexibility, while being able to withstand the incredible amounts of stress placed upon them. It is estimated that each stride of an adult places 900 pounds of pressure per square inch on the bottom of the foot. Seven of these bones form the compact arrangement of the ankle, or tarsus, and the heel.

Calcaneus;

The calcaneus bone forms the lower, outer part of the ankle and extends downward to form the heel. It is responsible for bearing much of the immediate stress placed upon the foot during walking and running. **The outside (knife) edge is the striking implement used when executing a Side Kick.**

Femur;

The femur is the longest bone in the body, and composes the upper leg, or thigh. The upper portion of the femur articulates with the acetabulum, the large circular cavity on each side of the pelvis, to form the ball and socket joint at the hip. The bottom portion of the femur articulates with the tibia and fibula, and the patella (knee cap) to form the knee joint. Each femur directly bears the weight of the entire upper body. **The femur provides support to the lower leg bones (tibia and fibula), at the junction of the knee joint, which lend direct support to the calcaneus bone. The head of the femur also connects to the pelvis.**

Fibula;

The fibula is the smaller of the two bones of the lower leg. It articulates at each end with the parallel tibia, at its upper portion with the femur to form the knee joint, and at its lower portion with the bones of the ankle, or tarsus. The fibula is so named

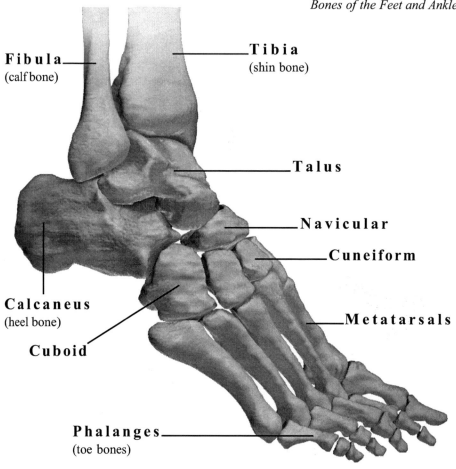

Fibula (calf bone)

Tibia (shin bone)

Talus

Navicular

Cuneiform

Calcaneus (heel bone)

Cuboid

Metatarsals

Phalanges (toe bones)

because it serves as a brace for the lower leg. **The fibula along with the tibia, lend direct support to the calcaneus bone, which is the striking implement used when executing a Side Kick.**

Knee;

The knee is the hinge like joint formed by the lower end of the femur, the upper ends of the tibia and fibula, and the patella (kneecap). The knee is a joint, which is subjected to tremendous lateral stress during normal activity and is guarded by a number of ligaments to help lend it support. Even so, however, the increased stresses placed upon this joint during extreme athletic activity, which require the individual to alter directions rapidly, the knee often bears the brunt of intolerable shearing forces. Such incidences often result in torn ligaments within the knee, which require corrective surgery. Proper technique and attention to detail must be utilized at all times in order to avoid injuring yourself during the execution of any technique. **The knee due to its unique structure and function, and when utilized correctly, vastly increases the speed and power generated in the execution of a Side Kick.**

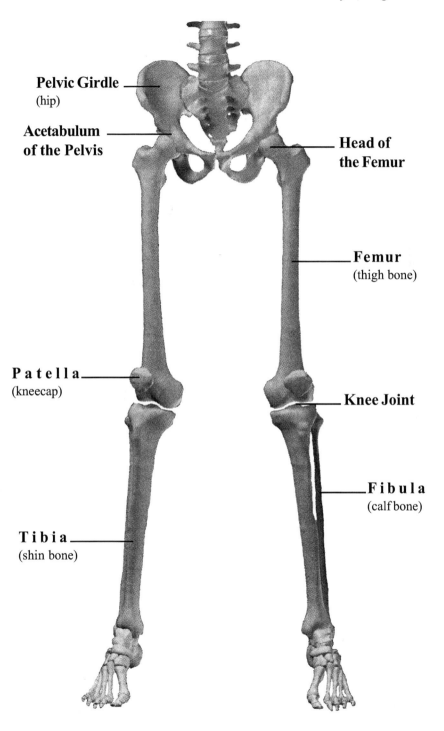

Pelvic Girdle
(hip)

Acetabulum
of the Pelvis

Head of
the Femur

Femur
(thigh bone)

P a t e l l a
(kneecap)

Knee Joint

F i b u l a
(calf bone)

T i b i a
(shin bone)

Patella;

The patella or kneecap is a small bone of the knee joint, which resembles an inverted teardrop. The patella is connected to the joint by a series of ligaments.

Pelvis;

The pelvis creates the basin of the lower abdominal cavity. It articulates with the sacrum in the back, and thereby connects to the rest of the vertebral column, and also to the legs through the ball and socket joint formed by the two acetabula of the pelvis and the head of each femur. **The pelvis is the connecting link between the actions of the upper and lower body.**

Phalanges;

The bones of the toes are known as phalanges. Each toe has three phalanges, with the exception of the large toe, which has only two. Toes and ankles are the most common self-inflicted injuries when kicking. Keeping your toes back, and out of the way, and your foot tight upon impact will greatly reduce the risk of injury. **The toes provide balance and stability in all activities that involve moving on your feet.**

Tibia;

The tibia is the primary bone of the two in the lower leg. Also called the shinbone, the tibia bears most of the weight. Its upper portion articulates with the parallel fibula, patella and the femur at the knee joint. Its lower portion articulates with the fibula and the talus of the ankle. **The tibia along with the fibula lend direct support to the calcaneus bone, which is the striking implement used when executing a Side Kick.**

MUSCLES:

The muscles and joints of the legs provide strength and stability for the body. These muscles serve to transmit the weight of the body and provide power for such common activities as walking, running and jumping. They also absorb the cumulative impact of those activities. The leg bones are girded on all sides by sets of powerful muscles that allow the legs to bend (flexion) and straighten (extension) as well as move outward from the body (abduction) and inward (adduction). Some of these muscles are relatively long and participate in more than one type of movement. The thigh consists of the body's largest bone, the femur, which is bound on all sides by sets of powerful muscles.

The calf, ankle, and foot are controlled largely by a series of muscles and tendons that function as a single biomechanical unit. These muscles work together to lift or lower the heel for virtually any activity that involves locomotion. All of the parts of the lower leg are interconnected. For example, when you stand on your toes, you can feel the muscles in the back of your calf doing most of the work. Because of its structure, and because it absorbs the impact from activities like running and jumping, the lower leg is subject to more exercise related injuries than any other area of the body. These problems range from bunions and blisters to stress fractures and ankle sprains, the most common sports injury of all.

The feet and toes are essential elements in body movement. They bear and propel the weight of the body during walking and running, and help to maintain balance during changes of body position. The foot can adapt itself to different surfaces and

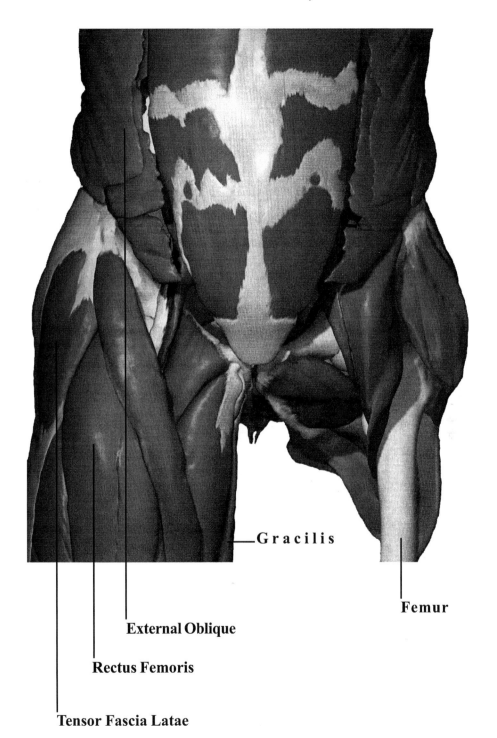

Gracilis

Femur

External Oblique

Rectus Femoris

Tensor Fascia Latae

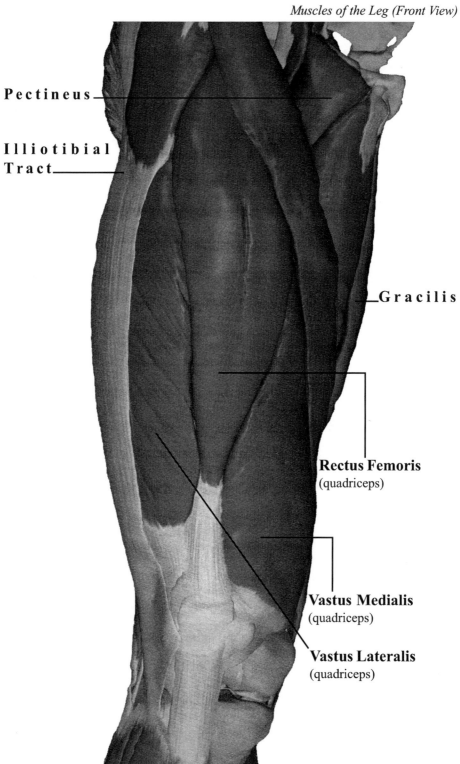

Pectineus

Illiotibial
Tract

Gracilis

Rectus Femoris
(quadriceps)

Vastus Medialis
(quadriceps)

Vastus Lateralis
(quadriceps)

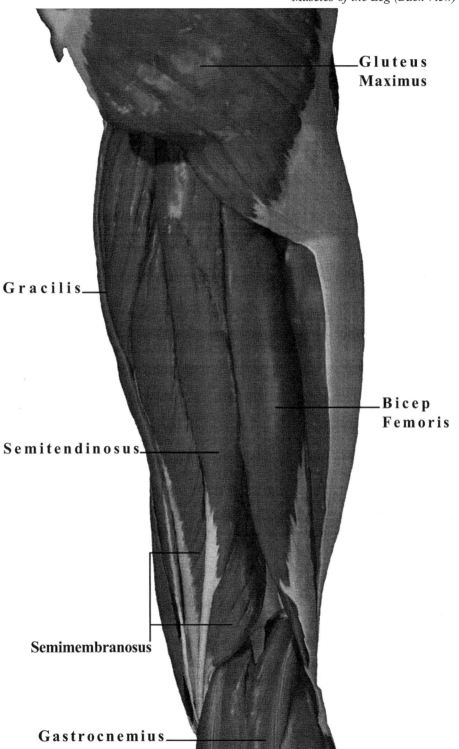

Gluteus
Maximus

Gracilis

Bicep
Femoris

Semitendinosus

Semimembranosus

Gastrocnemius

19

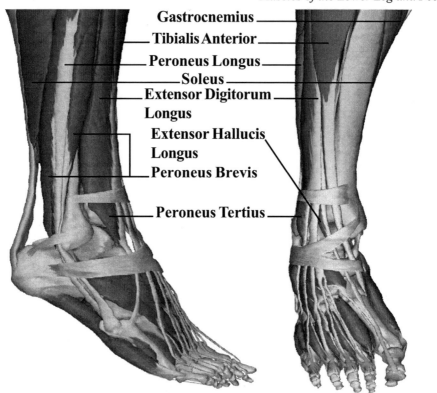

Gastrocnemius
Tibialis Anterior
Peroneus Longus
Soleus
Extensor Digitorum Longus
Extensor Hallucis Longus
Peroneus Brevis
Peroneus Tertius

absorb mechanical shocks as well. Each foot has about thirty-three muscles, some of which are attached to the lower leg.

Bicep Femoris;

The bicep femoris muscle runs from the tuberosity of the ischium down to the back of the head of the fibula. This muscle flexes the lower leg at the knee joint and also abducts or rotates the tibia outward. **This muscle bends the lower leg at the knee joint when entering into the "Coil" position, as well as, during the act of "Recoiling" after kicking.**

Extensor Digitorum Longus;

The extensor digitorum longus muscle arises from the tibia and the front of the fibula, and runs down into the foot and the toes. This muscle extends the toes and flexes the foot toward the leg. **This muscle assists in pushing off the floor with your toes when you begin to raise your knee into the "Coil" position. It also flexes the foot toward your knee in order to obtain the proper foot position for the Side Kick.**

Extensor Hallucis Longus;

The extensor hallucis longus muscle lies deep in the lower leg and extends down to the big toe. This muscle extends the big toe and assists in flexing the foot. **As with the extensor digitorum longus, this muscle assists in pushing off the floor with your big toe when you begin to raise your knee into the "Coil" position.**

It also flexes the foot toward your knee in order to obtain the proper foot position for the Side Kick.

External Oblique;

The external oblique muscle runs along the side of the torso and partially on the front from the lower ribs to the rectus, the pubis bone, and iliac crest of the hip. This muscle assists the rectus abdominus muscle in flexing the spine when the trunk twists or turns. **This muscle assists with the flexing of the spine and twisting of the upper body when entering into the "Coil" position to execute the Side Kick.**

Flexor Digitorum Longus;

The flexor digitorum longus muscle runs deep in the lower leg from the middle of the tibia to underneath the foot to the toes. This muscle assists to flex the toes during the final push off in walking or running. **As with the extensor digitorum longus and the extensor hallucis longus, this muscle assists in pushing off the floor with your toes when you begin to raise your knee into the "Coil" position.**

Gastrocnemius;

The gastrocnemius muscle runs from the back of the knee to the ankle to form the calf muscle. This muscle propels the body when walking, running or jumping. It raises the heel, which lifts the body. It also assists, though minimally, in flexing the knee joint. **This muscle assists the bicep femoris in bending the lower leg at the knee joint when entering into the "Coil" position, as well as returning to the coil position after kicking. It is also responsible for raising the heel of your foot off the ground when moving into the coil position.**

Gemelli;

The gemelli are two small muscles of the hip. The muscles arise from the spine and insert into the upper edge of the thighbone. These muscles help rotate the thigh. **This muscle helps rotate the thigh when turning to enter into the coil position. They also come into play by rotating the thigh immediately prior to, and immediately after the execution of the Side Kick.**

Gluteus Maximus;

We sit on the largest and most powerful muscle in our body, the gluteus maximus. This muscle powerfully extends the thigh at the hip joint and moves it away from the body, as when walking or running. **When used properly, this is the one muscle that produces the most power when executing the Side Kick. The flexing of this muscle is what helps propel your foot toward your opponent when executing a Side Kick.**

Gluteus Medius;

The gluteus medius runs from the outer portion of the pelvis, up to the crest of the pelvis. The gluteus medius is partially covered by the gluteus maximus. It moves the thigh outward and rotates it, as when walking or running. It keeps the torso upright during walking when one foot is touching the ground and the other is not. **This muscle assists in the execution and retraction of the Side Kick by moving the thigh outward and rotating it as you kick.**

Gracilis;

The gracilis muscle lies on the inside of the femur and begins at the pubic arch and runs down towards the inside of the tibia or shinbone. This muscle brings the knee up and pulls it across the front, toward the middle of the body. It also assists in rotation of the leg. **This is the primary muscle utilized when bringing the knee up into the "Coil" position.**

Iliopsoas;

The iliopsoas runs from deep in the back of the abdomen towards its insertion on the back of the femur. This muscle flexes the hip and assists in abduction and outward rotation of the hip. **This muscle assists in the execution and retraction of the Side Kick by moving the hip outward and rotating it as you kick.**

Iliotibial Tract;

The iliotibial tract begins at the upper edge of the femur and ends where it inserts into the condyle of the tibia. It acts almost like a ligament, by helping mainly to stabilize the knee joint, but also acts in flexing (bending) and extending (straightening) the knee. **This muscle assists in bending and straightening the knee during the "Coil," actual execution of the Side Kick, and the "Recoil."**

Pectineus;

The pectineus muscle lies on the front of the upper and middle part of the thigh. This muscle flexes and moves the thigh towards the body and rotates it towards the center. **This muscle helps flex the hip creating added force (not speed) to the Side Kick.**

Peroneus Brevis;

The peroneus brevis muscle runs along the outside of the lower half of the fibula or lower leg. This muscle works with the peroneus longus to extend the foot. **This muscle helps extend the foot as when pushing off the floor to move into the "Coil" position.**

Peroneus Longus;

The peroneus longus muscle runs along the upper part of the outside of the fibula or lower leg. This muscle works with the peroneus brevis to extend the foot. **This muscle, along with the peroneus brevis, helps extend the foot as when pushing off the floor to move into the "Coil" position.**

Peroneus Tertius;

The peroneus tertius runs from the lower third of the fibula downward and slightly forward, across the ankle and inserts into the little toe. This muscle provides dorsiflexion and eversion of the foot. **This muscle helps the foot maintain its proper position in order to execute the Side Kick.**

Plantaris;

The plantaris muscle runs from the lower end of the femur down to a small area on the bottom of the calcaneus or heel bone. This muscle works with the gastrocnemius to extend the ankle if the foot is free, and bend the knee if the foot is fixed, as when walking. **This muscle assists the gastrocnemius muscle to bend the knee when your foot is in the proper position for executing a Side Kick.**

Popliteal Region;

The popliteal muscle starts from the femur and the ligament behind the knee joint and extends down to the shaft of the tibia or shinbone. This muscle assists in rotating the tibia and is used when bending the knee. **This muscle is used when bending the knee for coiling and recoiling.**

Quadriceps;

The quadriceps consists of four separate muscles. The rectus femoris, which runs from the ilium or hipbone down to the knee. This muscle flexes the hip joint and helps with hip joint abduction. The vastus lateralis is located halfway down the outside of the thigh, this muscle extends the knee, but it needs the vastus medialis in order to give a straight pull to the knee. The vastus intermedius lies between the vastus medialis and the vastus lateralis, and beneath the rectus femoris. This muscle extends the knee with its pull directly upward on the patella. And finally the vastus medialis, which is located above the knee, on the top of the thigh. This muscle extends the knee with the assistance of the vastus lateralis. These muscles cover the front and sides of the femur or thigh, and work together as a primary extensor of the knee. The rectus femoris muscle extends the leg at the knee joint and flexes the thigh at the hip joint. **The four-quadriceps muscles work together to straighten the knee when executing the Side Kick.**

Semimembranosus;

The semimembranosus muscle begins in the tuberosity of the ischium or underneath and back of the pelvis, and runs two-thirds of the way down the back of the thigh to the outer condyle of the femur or upper leg, just above the knee. This muscle extends the thigh and assists with the inward rotation of the hip joint. It also provides flexion and inward rotation for the knee. **This muscle along with the semitendinosus assists in straightening the thigh when executing the Side Kick and with rotating the knee inward.**

Semitendinosus;

The semitendinosus muscle begins in the ischium or bottom and back of the pelvis, and runs two-thirds of the way down the middle of the back of the thigh. It is considered one of the hamstring muscles. This muscle flexes the lower leg and extends the thigh at the hip joint. It also provides flexion and inward rotation for the knee. **This muscle along with the semimembranosus assists in straightening the thigh when executing the Side Kick and with rotating the knee inward.**

Soleus;

The soleus muscle is located on the back of the lower leg and runs from the upper part of the fibula down to the middle portion of the calcaneus or heel bone. This muscle is used to point the foot or raise the heel, which lifts the body. **This muscle raises the heel off the floor when bringing the knee up to the "Coil" position.**

Tensor Fascia Latae;

The tensor fascia latae muscle is located on the outer front corner of the ilium or hipbone. It connects the ilium to the tissues of the outer thigh. This muscle flexes, abducts, and medially rotates the thigh. **This muscle assists in the execution and retraction of the Side Kick by moving the hip outward and rotating it as you kick.**

Tibialis Anterior;

The tibialis anterior muscle sits on the front of the tibia, and originates from the outside of the tibia below the knee and runs down into the foot. This muscle controls the descent of the foot during walking after the heel strikes the ground. **This muscle assists in keeping your foot in the proper position in order to execute the Side Kick.**

Tibialis Posterior;

The tibialis posterior muscle originates from the back of the tibia, behind the knee, and runs down into the foot. This muscle flexes the foot and, working with the tibialis anterior, turns the sole of the foot inward. It is the strongest support for the arch of the foot. **This muscle is responsible for adding "spring" to your foot when stepping or running.**

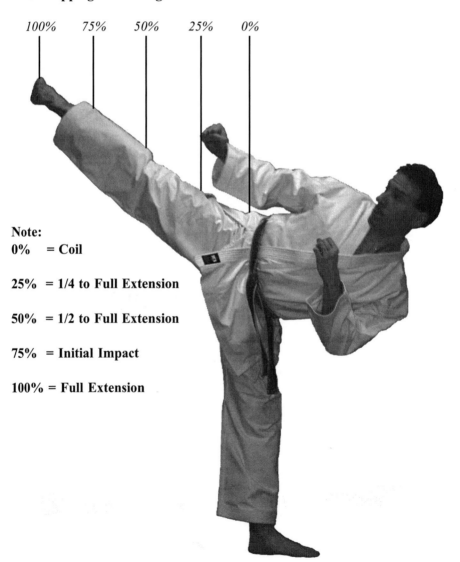

Note:

0%   = Coil

25%   = 1/4 to Full Extension

50%   = 1/2 to Full Extension

75%   = Initial Impact

100% = Full Extension

Warm Up and Stretching

Although stretching is perhaps the single greatest activity that you can perform to improve your kicking (other than utilizing proper technique), I am not going to go into great detail on the types of stretches to perform. Instead I will try and give you a firm understanding on the do's and don'ts of proper stretching. So without further delay, let's get started.

It is a well-known fact that active people tend to lead fuller more productive lives due to better health. Their endurance and stamina are greater not only during exercise, but also during normal everyday activities; such as climbing stairs, walking, doing normal household chores, etc. Medical research has shown us over the years that poor health is directly related to our increasingly sedentary life-style.

Research has also shown us that exercise, done at any age, retards the aging factor and allows our bodies to become healthier and more resistant to disease. It is obvious that as we become less active, we begin to lose not only our physical strength, but our mental strength as well. Therefore, our ability to utilize our bodies potential is greatly diminished. However, we can regain that potential and more through a correct and consistent stretching and training program.

Without a daily regiment of stretching and physical conditioning, our bodies become atrophied and weak with stored up tension, both physical and mental. Let's face it, regardless of how out of shape you are from lack of physical activity and poor eating habits, your body's potential to recover from this mistreatment and in fact flourish to new levels of health and increased physical abilities, is nothing short of phenomenal.

What does stretching do for your body? Well primarily it keeps your muscles and connective tissue flexible and more resilient to injury. It also prepares your body for more vigorous activity. Similar to starting your automobiles engine in cold weather and allowing it to idle for several minutes before driving. This idling period allows the engine of your car to warm up before the more strenuous demands of driving are placed upon it. Stretching is the idling period for your body. Stretching is essential to any martial art or combat sport, if you wish to perform at your optimum level, whether that is in the dojo, on the street, or in competition. Stretching in and of itself is easy to do, when performed correctly and consistently, and should take you between 25 to 35 minutes depending upon your level of fitness.

However, when performed incorrectly, it can actually cause injuries and impede your progress. It is for this reason that I recommend that you utilize your head when stretching and take your time. Perform the stretches correctly and slowly for the best results. Stretch at your own pace, not someone else's.

A regular program of correct stretching, will help you avoid injuries and will allow you to perform to the best of your abilities. Stretching, when performed correctly should not be painful. You should be able to feel the stretch, as it is performed in a slow, relaxing manner. Your body should not be tense nor should you force your body when stretching. Stretching should be a relaxing and warming up process, which takes place before performing a strenuous exercise.

Do Not make stretching a strenuous exercise. Your goal to achieve when stretching should be to reduce tension in the muscles, which will allow you to stretch further. Which in turn improves your level of flexibility. For the best results, stretch before and after participating in any strenuous activity, in addition to a daily stretching routine. A good stretching program can be adjusted to suit the needs of the individual. Certain characteristics to keep in mind when developing a stretching program are; type of activity involved in, personal goals, body type, current level of flexibility, and most important, your current physical condition.

Anyone who actively participates in a correct stretching program on a regular basis can become more flexible and improve their overall physical conditioning. You don't have to be able to perform the splits or be the reincarnation of Bruce Lee in order to gain flexibility, but you do have to have the desire and the willingness to train on a daily basis, and perhaps more importantly, you must learn to be patient with yourself.

Do's and Don'ts of Stretching:

Do's:
1. Wear loose fitting, yet comfortable clothing that will not impede movement and will keep your body warm in cold or inclement weather.
2. Perform a light exercise to get your body warmed up such as jumping rope, running in place, etc.
3. Hold each stretch for 10 to 30 seconds. Relax. Then go a little farther into your stretch and hold for another 10 to 30 seconds.
4. Keep your breathing slow and under control.
5. Keep track of the time during each stretch by slowly counting to yourself.
6. When your are performing the stretch correctly, you should feel a mild tension in the muscles. It should not be painful.
7. Take your time when stretching.
8. Stretch every day for 25 to 35 minutes.
9. Pay attention to your body and what it tells you.

Don'ts:
1. Bounce up and down while stretching.
2. Over stretch to where it becomes painful.
3. Hold your breath while stretching.

Perhaps the greatest example of what a daily program of stretching can do for you is brought to us from the animal kingdom. The most dangerous and skillful hunters are without a doubt the cats. From the regal "king of the beasts" on the plains of Africa, to our own domestic house cats. No other animal displays such a tremendous combination of flexibility, agility, and strength as the cat. Watch them and learn. Remember that Rome wasn't built in a day, and neither shall you.

Basic Principles of Movement
for the Back Leg Side Kick

In this chapter, I will give you a basic understanding of the kicking principles involved in the correct execution of a Side Kick. Although a lot of these principles are the same for the other primary kicks and their variations, there are others that are exclusive only to the Back Leg Side Kick and its variations. Study each one of these in detail until you know them inside and out. The more you know about a kick, the better you will be able to execute it.

Striking Implement:

The striking implement utilized in executing any Side Kick, is the outside (knife) edge of the heel or calcaneus bone. This bone extends down from the ankle to form the heel.

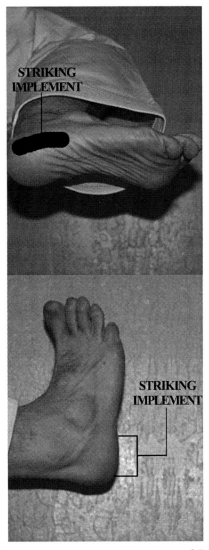

When a Side Kick is properly executed, with the outside (knife) edge of the heel as the striking implement, the bones and muscles of the ankle, lower leg, upper leg and hip provide additional support upon impact with the target. As you can see, in the photographs on the right, hitting with the sole of the foot or your toes, would result in little more than a push or hard slap, when executing a Side Kick.

Remember, the idea is not to inflict damage upon yourself, but rather to your intended target when executing a Side Kick. Therefore, you must constantly be aware of your foot position and proper striking surface every time you kick, even if you are only kicking air.

One way to produce a greater amount of force is to utilize a smaller surface area when striking your intended target. Let's say for the sake of argument that you can deliver a total of 100 lbs. of force to your target, and that the surface area of the outside (knife) edge of your heel is equal to 2 square inches. If you strike the target correctly with the outside (knife) edge of your heel, you will be able to deliver 50 lbs. of pressure per square inch. However, if you strike the target incorrectly with your entire foot, which has a surface area of say 20 square inches, then you would be striking your target with 5 lbs. of pressure per square inch. Do you see what the difference is between striking with the correct surface area of the foot and the incorrect surface area? Not quite sure, let me put it to you this way. Try hammering a nail into a piece of wood using the pointed end of the nail to make contact with the board first, and then hammering on the head of the nail. Then take another nail and lay it on its side and try hammering it into the wood?

Now do you see the relevancy of striking with the correct surface area? Although the amount of force exerted against your opponent in both cases are equal, the pressure exerted upon the target struck correctly with the heel is five times greater than if you used the entire surface area of your foot. When you strike the intended target with to large a surface area, you are dissipating the force over a wider surface area resulting in a push or surface strike, rather than a penetrating impact. This greatly reduces the effectiveness of your kick.

Target Areas:

I define the target area as, the general location of a vital or vulnerable point on the human body. For the greatest effectiveness with the Side Kick in combat, you want to strike a particular vital or vulnerable point every time you strike your opponent. This will most likely deter any continued attack from your opponent by causing pain and/or injury. However, this is not always possible as very few individuals are going to stand there and let you hit them. They are going to be moving, blocking, dodging, and perhaps more importantly, trying to hit you back. Therefore, you want to be able to strike your opponent the most effective and efficient way that you can.

One component of that is a thorough knowledge of the vital or vulnerable points of the human body. Not only is this knowledge important to inflict damage upon your opponent (only when absolutely necessary), but also to enable you to avoid such damage being inflicted upon yourself. I am not going to discuss in detail the vital or vulnerable points in this book. However, I am going to list the general target areas and the vital or vulnerable points that lie within those areas that you will want to strike with the Side Kick. For more detailed information on vital or vulnerable points, please refer to the recommended reading section at the back of this book.

The effects of striking each vital or vulnerable point vary drastically depending on the accuracy, direction, speed, and power utilized when striking them. Another factor that has to be taken into consideration is the human factor. Each individual is vastly different from the next and each person is going to react differently when struck. Some people may go down from the lightest of blows, while still others will merely shake off your strongest blows and keep coming at you. Which is a very good reason why you should have a thorough understanding of vital and vulnerable points.

Be prepared for any and all eventualities. Because serious injury or even death may result from forceful blows to these vital or vulnerable points, you must exercise extreme caution when practicing with a partner, and you should never actually strike any of these areas with even the lightest blows in practice. If you are called upon to strike these areas in self-defense, you should only use full force to save one's life.

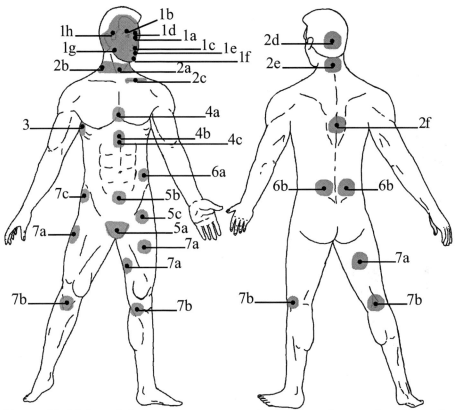

Along with this knowledge comes great responsibility, not only to one's self, but also to those around you. **Never Use Excessive Force!**

1. **Facial Area:** This target area encompasses the nose (1a), orbital bones (1b), the philtrum (1c), glabella (1d), mouth (1e), point of chin (1f), the jaw (1g), and the temple (1h).

2. **Neck Area:** This target area encompasses the throat (2a), side of neck (2b), the collarbone (2c), the occipital bone (2d), the 3rd intervertebral space (2e), and the spine (2f).

3. **Armpit Area:** This target area encompasses the ribs below the armpit and to the side of the chest.

4. **Lower Chest/Upper Abdomen Area:** This target area encompasses the sternum (4a), xiphoid process (4b), and the solar plexus (4c).

5. **Lower Abdomen Area:** This target area encompasses the pubic region and groin (5a), the lower abdomen (5b), and the front of the hip where the leg joins the pelvic bone (5c).

6. **Lower Side Area:** This target area encompasses primarily the ribs located just above the crest of the hipbone (6a) and the kidneys (6b).

7. **Leg Area:** This target area encompasses the front, back, inside and outside of the thigh (7a), the front, back, inside and outside of the knee (7b), and the hip joint (7c).

Each one of these vital or vulnerable points can be struck utilizing the Side Kick.

Stability:

For the purpose of the material presented in this book, stability is defined as, "A person's ability to stand upon any given surface in a controlled and capable manner." For example you would have an easier time executing a kick on a hard flat surface such as cement or pavement, than you would if you were standing on gravel or ice. Sometimes it is necessary to create a very stable position or stance, such as when delivering a powerful kick.

Other times it is important to be in an unstable position, such as moving quickly in order to avoid being hit. Therefore, a thorough understanding of the following principles will give you the ability to apply them on a daily basis, whether it be in practice, self-defense, or in competition. Several different factors contribute to one's stability such as your weight, height, center of gravity, equilibrium or balance, and your base of support. Let's take a look at each one of these factors.

Weight:

With all other factors being equal, a heavier person is generally speaking more stable than a lighter person. Consequently, a heavier person such as World Heavyweight Boxing Champion George Foreman would be harder to push off balance than a lighter person such as World Boxing Champion Oscar De LaHoya. It also stands to reason that Foreman is able to punch harder from his heavier and more solid position than De LaHoya is from his lighter and less solid position.

However, no one would argue the fact that De LaHoya, being a lighter weight fighter, has the advantage of being able to move and change direction quicker than the heavier Foreman. This is of course taking into consideration that all other factors involved are equal. I have seen some very big men that could move a lot faster and a lot smoother than their smaller counterparts.

Height and Center of Gravity:

Your center of gravity is defined as being located approximately 2 to 3 inches below your belly button and in the center of your body when standing perfectly straight with correct posture, and your feet flat on the floor. This of course varies from person to person and also upon their general body type. Women tend to have a lower center of gravity than men, and individuals with heavier legs have a lower center of gravity than someone with lighter legs. The closer one's center of gravity is to the ground or base of support, the greater their increase in stability.

You can easily change your center of gravity by bending your knees and squatting down to lower it, or by standing on your toes to raise it. You can even move your center of gravity outside your body by bending over at the waist and touching your toes. Generally speaking, the taller you are the less stability you have, while the shorter you are the more stability you have. Ask yourself this question, which has more stability the giraffe or the hippopotamus?

Equilibrium:

Equilibrium is defined as a state of balance between opposing forces. A prime example of equilibrium is a figure skaters ability to stand upon the toes of their skates while spinning their entire body into a tightly controlled blur of motion and then stopping without any outwards signs of loss of balance or equilibrium. For equilibrium to exist, your center of gravity must be centered over your base of support throughout the entire sequence of events involved when executing the Side Kick, or any other athletic endeavor. Failure to maintain equilibrium will result in a loss of balance, and can result in a slight case of disorientation. Either of which could prove disastrous in a self-defense or tournament situation.

Base of Support:

Your base of support is described as the area of the feet upon which the weight of your body is supported, along with the space between your feet. For example,

(A) if you were standing flat footed with both feet on the ground and directly beneath your shoulders, your base of support would not only include both feet, but also the space between them.

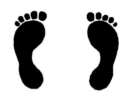

(B) If you were standing on the toes of both feet, your base of support would include the surface area of your feet that are in direct contact with the ground and the space between them.

And

(C) if you were balancing on the ball of one foot, your base of support would be the surface area covered by the ball of your base foot.

Generally speaking, the greater the surface area of your feet that is in direct contact with the ground, and the wider the stance, the greater your base of support.

Therefore, after taking all of these factors into consideration, it stands to reason that the heavier, shorter individual is more stable during the execution of a punch when both feet are on the ground, than the lighter taller individual is when executing a kick and balancing on one leg. Does this mean that you are better off punching than kicking? Of course not, it simply means that the skills needed to kick effectively take a lot more time, effort, and attention to detail than those skills needed to punch effectively.

This is one of the reasons why so many people tend to neglect their kicking skills in favor of the easier learned punching and grappling skills. Your stance when fighting should be unstable in that you should not be set in one position, you should be constantly moving in order to avoid an attack while positioning yourself to effectively attack your opponent.

If your stance is too wide, you will sacrifice mobility as well as telegraphing any kick that you may attempt. This in effect makes you a sitting duck. If your stance is too short, you will have lost balance and stability. The ideal stance is to keep your feet shoulder width apart in length and about 4 to 8 inches apart in width.

Balance:

Although the previous section on stability also included information on equilibrium or balance, this section is devoted to balance as it applies to the execution of a kick. If you do not have good balance when kicking, not only is your kick going to be ineffective, but you may have put yourself in a dangerous situation by overextending or "reaching" with your kicking leg, losing your balance all together, and possibly even falling to the ground. In order to prevent this, you must follow these few simple points when executing your kick.

1. Your center of gravity must be centrally located over your base foot throughout the entire kicking sequence from start to finish.

2. In order to execute your kick, you are going to pivot on the ball of your base foot. However, the entire base foot must be in direct contact with the ground at the moment of impact, with your center of gravity in the middle of the foot, not over the ball, heel, inner or outer edge of the foot. After the initial contact is made, you will continue with the "Recoil" and then return the kicking foot to the starting position by once again pivoting on the ball of the base foot. You should never make contact with your target while balancing on the ball of your base foot. This incorrect technique is not only unstable, but it also causes a dramatic decrease in the effectiveness of the kick.

3. The position of your base foot is directly related to the effectiveness of maintaining your balance when kicking. For example, the inside edge of your base foot is facing at a 45-degree angle toward your opponent during the "Impact" phase of a Side Kick. Try performing the Side Kick with the toes of your base foot pointed at your opponent. Now try it with the outside edge of your foot facing toward your opponent. Did they work? How does your knee and hips feel?

4. And finally, don't forget the importance of that area of the body above your waist. I always find it amazing how many people forget about how important proper upper body position is to achieving and maintaining balance when kicking. Keep your head up and looking at your opponent, keep your back straight, and stop moving your arms around like a bird flapping its wings.

You'll be surprised at how much your kicks have improved by simply paying attention to these few things.

Alignment:

Your entire body should be aligned properly at the moment of impact in order to generate the maximum amount of power into the delivery of your kick upon its target. The proper body alignment at the moment of impact for the Side Kick is as follows. The kicking foot is parallel with the ground, and the outside (knife) edge of the heel should be the only part of your foot in contact with the target. The toes should be in a horizontal position, and pulled back toward the kicking leg knee, which not only exposes the outside (knife) edge of the heel for better contact, but also tightens the ankle. In this position, your big toe should be closer to your kicking leg knee, while your pinkie toe is closer to your opponent.

The lower leg, knee, and upper leg should all be in a straight line and supporting one another in order to increase the overall effectiveness of the kick. The kicking leg hip, shoulder, back, and the head should all be in a straight line with the heel. The inside edge of your base leg foot is facing at a 45-degree angle toward your opponent, with the heel closer to your opponent than your toes. Your bases leg should be straight. This will have the effect of putting your entire body behind the kick, where the culmination of muscular speed, strength, and proper technique combine to deliver the generated force into your target along a straight and even "Path of Trajectory."

Sequence of Movement:

What this means is that the correct sequence of movements from the beginning stages of the kick, to "Impact" and subsequent "Recoil," should be followed in one smooth continuous motion in order to achieve the maximum effectiveness in your kick. In order to do this however, you must first work upon each individual section of the kick until you can effectively flow from one section of the kick to the other, without any noticeable pauses or breaks between them. Even though the Side Kick should be performed in one fluid motion, there are two distinct and separate sections to this kick. The first is the delivery of the kick from "Fighting Position" to "Impact," and the second is the retraction or "Recoil" after delivering the kick, which goes from "Impact" back to your original starting position. Combine the two, but keep them separate.

Accuracy:

No matter how perfectly you execute your Side Kick, it isn't going to do you one ounce of good unless you can hit your intended target. Imagine going out to war and being equipped with the biggest most powerful rifle you can get, and then not being able to hit your target. Now combine that with the fact that the guy you are fighting against is equipped with a .22 caliber rifle and the ability to hit a dime at 100 yards. Who do you think is going to survive that encounter? There are several factors involved in obtaining accurate kicks such as eye contact, proper technique, muscular control or coordination, breath control, conditioning, and most importantly, proper practice.

Eye Contact:

Your eyes should remain in constant contact with your opponent at all times. The focus of your attention should be like a flashlight on your opponent's chest, while your peripheral vision encompasses everything else from his head to his hands and down to his feet. Be careful not to focus your eyes like a laser beam on one single point, this can cause a delayed reaction time to incoming attacks and can also telegraph your intentions to your opponent.

Practice Proper Technique:

The ability to kick proficiently is not instinctive, it is a learned activity that takes years of study and constant practice to perfect. I cannot stress this simple fact enough, "Pay Attention To Detail and Practice!" The kicks presented in this book have been explained in precise detail so that you can learn the proper technique for executing them as efficiently and as accurately as possible. Practice and study the material in this book until it becomes second nature.

Muscular Control or Coordination:

This is the ability to control ones own body during physical activities such as kicking. This is not an easy skill to learn, and it takes a considerable amount of practice in order to utilize it effectively. The best method that I know of to improve your muscular control for kicking, is to perform the entire kicking sequence in slow motion until the point of impact, at which point you hold that position for approximately five seconds tensing your entire body during that time. After the five seconds are over, relax the entire body and slowly continue with the "Recoil" returning to your original starting position. This should be performed at least 10 times prior to and at the end of every kicking session. Another variation of this technique is to tense all of your muscles during the entire time you are performing this exercise. This is called Dynamic Tension training and is very effective.

Breathing:

You should never hold your breath when fighting. Breathing should be done normally by inhaling through your nose and exhaling through your mouth. Remember to keep your mouth closed when fighting. Don't open it or you may get a broken jaw for your trouble. At the exact moment that you make impact with your target, you will exhale sharply and tighten your entire body, this will add power to your kick.

Conditioning:

Physical conditioning is an absolute must if you want to perform these kicks to the best of your abilities. The better condition that you are in, the more that you will be able to do for a longer period of time before becoming fatigued. The harder you train, the easier it will become.

Strength:

Strength is the amount of muscular force that you can apply at any given time to a particular target. Don't confuse strength with power. Speed and strength are two sides of the same coin which when combined together create power. Pivoting of the hips and the turning of the body are two methods of applying strength to a kick with minimal muscular effort. I am sure you have heard of a boxer who uses only his arms when he punches, rather than utilizing his entire body. The same is also true of kicking, in that the majority of individuals kick only with their legs, rather than with their entire body.

Leg strength alone does not give any real strength to the kick. Granted there is some strength present, however it is minimal compared to the strength that can be delivered if the entire body is utilized in the execution of the kick. The positioning of your head, arms, hands, and upper body are also instrumental in increasing the strength of your kick.

Speed:

The only drawbacks to kicking are that although the leg is longer than the arm, it is relatively slower, and if you don't practice your kicking skills regularly they tend to deteriorate and lose their speed. Speed and strength are two side of the same coin, which when combined together creates power. To best explain this principle I like to use the analogy of a Lamborghini and a bulldozer.

Which one of the two is faster yet not very forceful? Which one is more forceful yet slower? Obviously, the Lamborghini is faster and the bulldozer is more forceful. Yet, if both of these vehicles started at the same time from one mile away and they both drove as fast as they could until they hit a brick wall at the end of that mile, which one would hit first, and second? And what would happen to them? Obviously, the Lamborghini traveling in excess of 200 plus miles per hour would strike the wall long before the much slower bulldozer. However, when it hit the wall it would totally destroy the car and I am sure would cause some minor damage to the wall.

The bulldozer on the other hand, would take a considerably longer amount of time to cover that distance in order to reach the wall. However, once it reached the wall, its greater strength would easily go through it. My whole point being that your body should be like the blinding speed of the Lamborghini as your foot travels to reach its target. However, at the moment of impact your foot and entire body should transform itself instantaneously from the blinding speed of the Lamborghini into the wall-crushing strength of the bulldozer. Immediately after impact, your entire body will return to the blinding speed of the Lamborghini in order to facilitate a faster "Recoil" and return to the starting position. A relaxed muscle is faster, while a tense or contracted muscle is slower yet stronger. Utilize this to your best advantage when executing these kicks.

Distance and Timing:

If the opponent is too far away, how are you going to hit him? If you execute a kick too slow or too fast, and your opponent moves, how are you going to hit him? If you attempt to execute a kick and your opponent is too close to you and jams the kick, how are your going to hit him? These are just a few of the problems that can be solved by creating the proper distance between you and your opponent and the utilization of proper timing. You cannot leave it up to chance or fate to create the perfect kicking distance between you and your opponent; you have to control the distance, and therefore the fight. Don't allow your opponent that opportunity.

Impact:

Impact is the culmination of all of the other principles and techniques performed correctly, in order to generate the maximum amount of force, and to transfer that power into your opponent at the precise moment of impact. If any one technique or principle is neglected, or applied improperly, then you will not be able to produce the maximum amount of force upon impact that you are capable of.

Retraction/Recoil:

Proper retraction or "Recoil" of the foot and leg after kicking is perhaps one of the most important movements you can make during the kicking sequence. To begin with, the faster your recoil is after striking your target, the more effective your kick is going to be. This is primarily due to the transfer of energy that is being delivered from your entire body through your leg and foot into the intended target at the moment of impact. The longer your striking implement is in contact with its target, the more energy that is reflected back into you rather than being transferred into the target.

Secondly, the longer you have your foot "hanging" in the air, the longer it is going to take you to follow up with another technique. It also allows your opponent the opportunity to grab your foot or leg and put you in a world of hurt. Unlike the movies where an actor can kick ten opponents all at once and never put his foot back on the ground, you should never attempt such a foolish stunt. Multiple kicks with one leg in the air can be effective, but only after years and years of devoted practice, and a cooperative opponent. As a general rule-of-thumb, as fast as your kick leaves the ground, it should be just as fast if not faster getting back down on the ground.

Visualization:

"Any sport is 95 percent mental, and anyone who tells you differently, doesn't know what he's talking about," Joe Fields, center for the New York Jets.

"Mind is everything, muscles are pieces of rubber," Paavo Nurmi, Olympic Gold Medallist.

Like I stated before, your mind controls your body. Therefore, you have to believe in yourself and your abilities, if you ever want to become more proficient than what you currently are. There are three separate and unique times that one should utilize visualization as an effective training tool. They are; before, during, and after every practice.

Before:

When you use visualization before practice you want to envision yourself performing the fastest, most powerful, most technically perfect kick you have ever done. Do not envision anything other than perfection. If you see yourself making mistakes or performing a kick poorly, then you will. If you see yourself doing your best then you will do your best. This is also referred to as positive thinking. It works, so use it. This should take anywhere from 5 to 15 minutes.

During:

As you are performing the kick, envision an imaginary target in front of you that you want to kick. Aim your kick to hit a certain target. Be aware of your body movement and position throughout the entire kicking sequence. Imagine your target being totally devastated by your kick. Concentrate!

After:

Use this time to reflect upon your workout and how well you did. Envision yourself doing even better the next time you practice. Answer this question, "If you don't believe in you, who will?"

Back Leg Side Kick

The Back Leg Side Kick is one of the ten primary kicks associated with Karate and/or Tae Kwon Do. Although it goes by many different names, the Side Kick, when performed properly, can be one of the more powerful kicks in the martial artist's arsenal. This section will go into minute detail over all areas and phases of the Back Leg Side Kick. Once this primary kick is mastered, all of the other variations of this primary kick will fall into place. Without any further ado, let's get started.

Fighting Stance:

Your fighting stance should be approximately shoulder width apart (1a) with the toes of your front or lead foot pointed directly at your opponent. The heel of your lead foot should be in a direct line (1b) with the heel of your rear foot. This allows you the opportunity to initiate a faster kick. Remember that the foot positions in this stance will actually change after you become comfortable executing this kick. At that time your feet will still be approximately shoulder width apart in length, however the heels will be about 4 to 8 inches apart, rather than in a straight line with one another.

The toes of your back or rear foot (1b) should be pointed away from your body at a 45-degree angle. For example, if your right foot were in the rear position, then the toes of that foot would be pointed to the right at a 45-degree angle. If the left foot were in the rear position, then the toes of your left foot would be pointed to the left at a 45-degree angle.

Your weight should be distributed over the balls of both feet and not over the entire surface area of the feet. This way your mobility is increased and you will be able to initiate a faster kick. The weight distribution over your feet should be approximately 55% over the lead leg and 45% over the rear leg. This also allows for faster movement when kicking or when evading your opponent's attack.

Your knees (2) should be slightly but not noticeably bent. The lead leg knee should be slightly bent over the lead leg foot in the direction of the toes. The same also holds true for the rear knee in the fact that it too should be slightly bent over the rear foot in the direction of the rear toes. The bending of the knees contributes to faster movement with the legs as they are not locked straight or rigid, and have better mobility when slightly bent rather than straight.

Your body (3) is facing at a 45-degree angle to your opponent. This presents a smaller target area facing toward your opponent. It also allows you better mobility moving forward toward your opponent, or backward away from your opponent. Additionally, it allows you quicker access to "off-set" your opponent by moving in the direction your body is facing.

Your hands (4a) and elbows (4b), should be held up like a boxer's, that is with the lead hand held up at head level and away from your face about 8 to 12 inches (toward your opponent). Your lead elbow should be tucked in along your side in order to protect your ribs and stomach area. Your rear hand is held up alongside your cheek or neck, with the palm of that hand facing toward your cheek. Your rear elbow is also tucked in along your side in order to protect your ribs and stomach area.

Your back (5) should be straight but not rigid and your lead shoulder should be raised up slightly in order to protect your chin.

Your head (6) is facing toward your opponent with the chin tucked down behind your upraised lead shoulder.

Your eyes (7) should focus like a flashlight on your opponent's chest to center your vision. At the same time, allow your peripheral vision to scan the rest of your opponent's body and therefore any movements he will make. A word of caution, **do not** become fixated on a particular spot or point of focus on your opponent. This becomes more of a hindrance than an asset when fighting.

Additionally, you should **never** take your eyes off your opponent for any reason. This mistake is quite common when first learning how to kick. A lot of students tend to watch their foot as it travels from the floor to its intended target. This is not only incorrect, but it can be very dangerous! Always maintain proper eye contact with your opponent. Remember the old saying, "Look before you leap?"

Fighting Position Foot Position
(Beginning)

Fighting Position Foot Position
(Advanced)

Note: In order to effectively utilize any technique, not just a kick, in combat you must become proficient in the following areas:

1. Create the appropriate distance without telegraphing any movements.

2. Initiate your technique without telegraphing the move to your opponent.

3. Utilize deception to your advantage throughout the entire confrontation.

4. Your must be as fast as possible, without sacrificing proper technique.

5. Never let your opponent know what you can do, or are about to do.

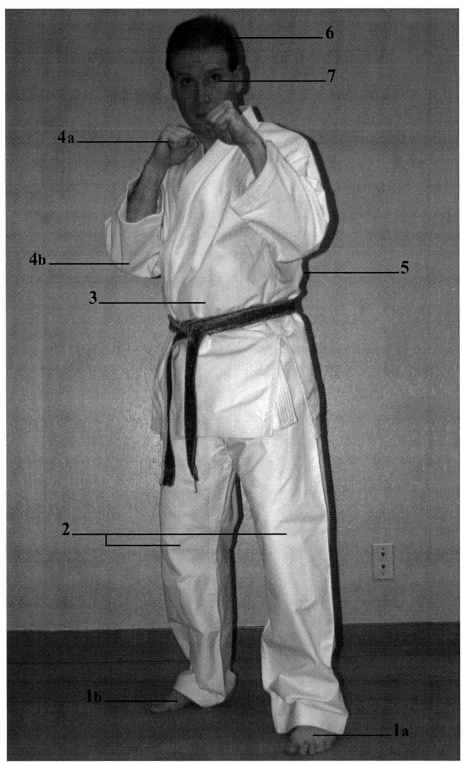

Fighting Position Front View

39

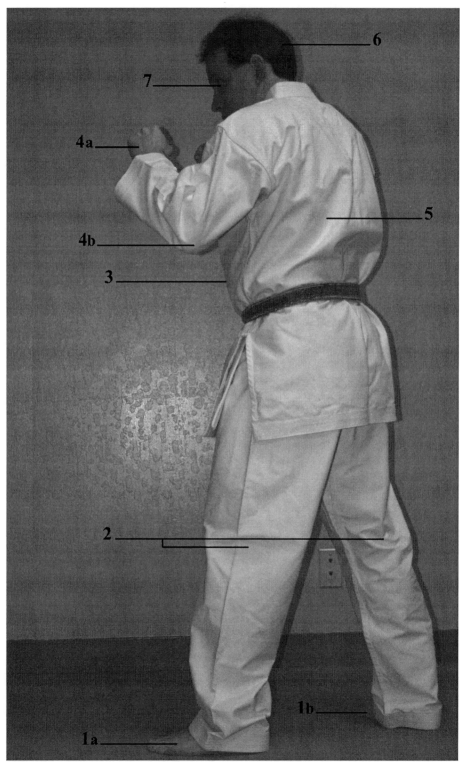

Fighting Position Side View

Raise Knee:

Although the initial raising of your kicking leg knee (10) in preparation to "Coil" and then execute the kick is rather simple to execute, its importance to the overall effectiveness of your kick should never be trivialized. This is done by simultaneously raising the heel of your kicking leg foot (11), while using the toes of your kicking foot to quickly push off the ground with the ball of your kicking foot (11).

After your kicking foot has left the ground, the muscles in your thigh contract to bring your kicking knee straight up in front of you and toward the center of your body, until your knee is at least waist high. At the same time you are raising your kicking knee (10) to the correct position, bring your kicking foot (11) back so that the bottom of your heel is momentarily touching the inside of your base leg knee.

Raise Knee
Foot Position

The outside (knife) edge of your kicking foot should be pointed down towards the ground with your toes flexed back towards your kicking leg knee. Your big toe will be closest to your kicking knee, and your pinkie toe will be closer to the ground. So that with your leg extended, the outside (knife) edge of your heel will make contact with the target, rather than your toes or the sole of your foot.

As you are bringing your kicking foot (11) up into position, you will be shifting 100% of your body weight onto your base leg foot (8), while your toes will remain pointing directly at your opponent. Your base leg will continue to bear 100% of your body weight from this point on, until your kicking foot returns back down on the ground during the "Return to Fighting Position" phase of the kick. Your base leg will remain straight with a slight bend in the base leg knee (9).

The front of your upper body (12a) is now facing at a slight angle to your opponent's right. With the kicking leg side of your body now closer to your opponent than your base leg side. Your back (12b) should remain straight but not rigid. You should not be bent over at the waist at this time.

Your hands (13a) and elbows (13b) should still be in relatively the same position as they were in your initial "Fighting Position."

Your head (14) is still up and facing toward your opponent so that you are now looking over the right hand side of your chest, rather than your base leg shoulder. Your chin should still be tucked down close to your chest and behind your lead hand. Your eyes (15) should still be centered on your opponent's chest.

Note: The act of raising your kicking knee up to the "Coil" position, should be done in a "lightning fast" manner by utilizing the muscles in the foot and ankle to initiate the action. The Seated Calf Machine exercise, which is explained in detail on page 182, is an excellent method of developing the muscles involved in this particular phase of the Side Kick.

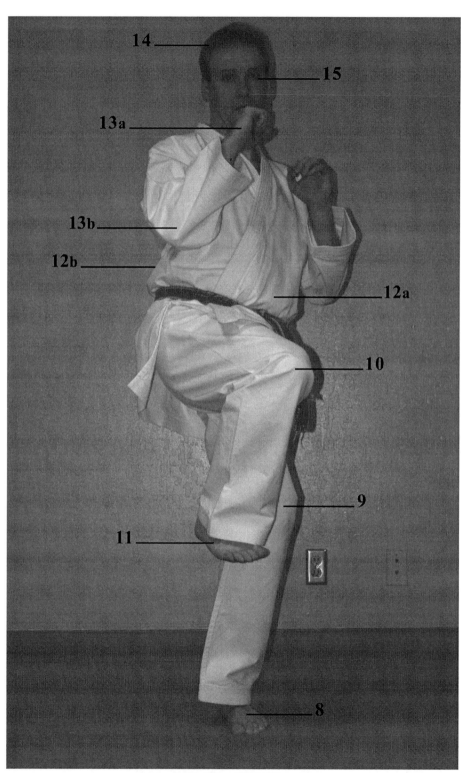

Raise Knee Front View

Raise Knee Side View

Coil:

Your base leg foot (16) should have moved approximately 90-degrees counterclockwise from where your toes are pointing at the 12 o'clock position, to where they are pointing at the 9 o'clock position and your heel is pointing at the 3 o'clock position. This is accomplished by pivoting on the ball of your base leg foot. Your base leg will continue to bear 100% of your body weight, until your kicking foot returns back down on the ground during the "Return to Fighting Position" phase of the kick. Your base leg will remain straight with a slight bend in the base leg knee (17).

Coil
Foot Position

Even though your body position has changed, your kicking leg knee (18) should be directly in front of your body, and at least waist high, although it is even more effective when raised to lower chest height. This is done by first raising the heel of your kicking leg foot as you quickly push off the ground with ball of your kicking foot. After your foot has left the ground, the muscles in your thigh contract to bring your knee up into the coil position.

Your kicking foot (19) should be slightly in front of your base leg and as high above the base leg knee as possible, while being tucked in close to your groin. The outside (knife) edge of your kicking foot should be pointed down towards the ground with your toes flexed back towards your kicking leg knee. Your big toe will be closest to your kicking knee, and your pinkie toe will be closer to the ground. So that with your leg extended, the outside (knife) edge of your heel will make contact with the target, rather than your toes or the sole of your foot. This provides a much tighter coil, which in turn gives your kick more power.

Too many martial artists are sacrificing a proper coil in order to get the kick to the target faster. Although it is true to a certain extent that a kick will get to the target faster without coiling, it is incorrect and can prove potentially harmful to the individual kicker. Proper technique should never be sacrificed for the sake of speed.

As you pivot on the ball of your base leg foot (16), you will also turn your body in a counterclockwise direction so that the kicking leg side of your body is now facing directly at your opponent. In this position, the front of your body (20a) is facing at a 90-degree angle to your opponent's right. Your back (20b) remains straight, but not rigid and does not bend over at the waist at this time. Your hands (21a) and elbows (21b), are also in relatively the same position as in (13a) and (13b).

Your head (22) remains in relatively the same position as in (14). Your eyes (23) are still focused on your opponent's chest like a flashlight, not a laser beam.

Note: Although some schools or styles advocate the use of the entire outside edge of your foot as the striking implement, I strongly disagree! Reach down and feel along the entire length of the outside edge of your foot. Where is the hardest and most durable portion of your foot, the base of your pinkie toe? the outside center of your foot? or, the outside edge of your heel?

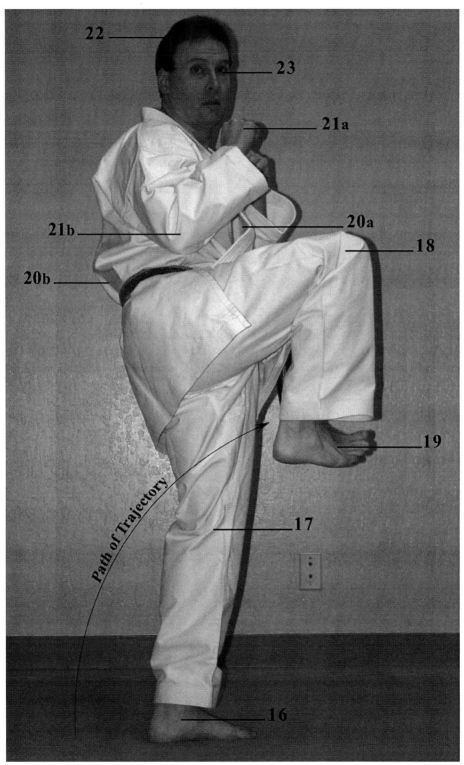

Coil Position Front View

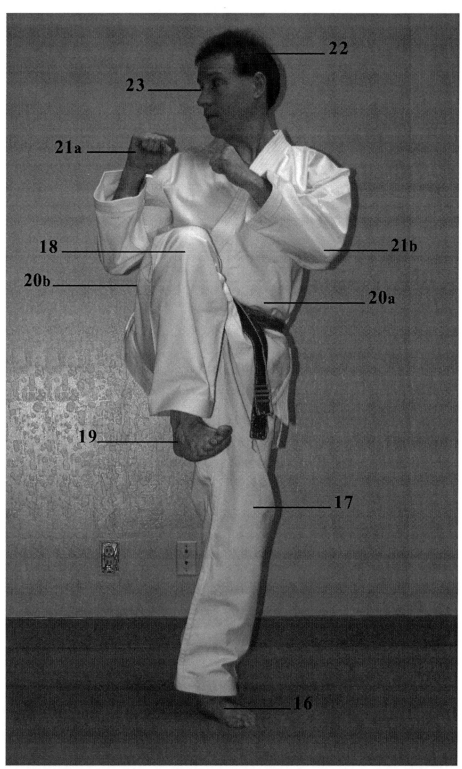

Coil Position Side View

Midway to Impact:

Your base leg foot (24) should have moved approximately 20-degrees counterclockwise by pivoting on the ball of your foot. Your base leg knee (25) is still slightly bent as your kicking foot (27) begins to travel along a straight and even "Path of Trajectory" from the "Coil" position, through its initial "Impact" with its target.

Midway to Impact
Foot Position

The entire bottom of your kicking foot (27) should be facing directly towards the ground, with the outside (knife) edge of your heel extended toward your opponent, and your toes flexed back toward your kicking leg knee. In this position, your big toe will be the closest to your kicking knee, while your pinkie toe will be closer to your opponent. So that with your leg extended, the outside (knife) edge of your heel will make contact with the target, rather than your toes or the sole of your foot. Although your toes and foot are flexed towards the kicking leg knee, do not flex them to the point of having your foot and ankle too tight. It should be a relaxed tension or flexion.

Your kicking leg knee (26) should be pointed to the side, and in this position, be almost parallel with the ground. Your knee will start to straighten out as it travels along a straight and even "Path of Trajectory" from the "Coil" position to "Impact."

The front of your body (28a) and your back (28b), should still be facing in relatively the same positions that they were in during the "Coil" position (20a) and (20b). However, your upper body should now start to lean over to your left, by bending over at the waist at almost a 45-degree angle in relation to your body's previous upright position. This position helps to facilitate an increased range of motion in order to properly execute the kick.

Your hands (29a), and elbows (29b), are still in relatively the same position as they were in the "Coil" position. That is with your hands up high around your chest and chin, and your elbows along side your rib cage.

Your head (30) is up and turned toward your opponent with your chin tucked in behind the kicking leg shoulder. Your eyes (31) should be looking over your kicking leg shoulder and focused on your opponent's chest.

Note: Although you want to make initial impact with your opponent when your kicking leg is at approximately 75% of full extension, your kicking foot will "strike through" the target and continue along its "Path of Trajectory," until your kicking leg reaches approximately 95% of full extension. You should never reach 100% of full extension as you then run the risk of damaging your knee. As soon as you reach full extension, immediately "Recoil" your kicking and get it back down on the ground.

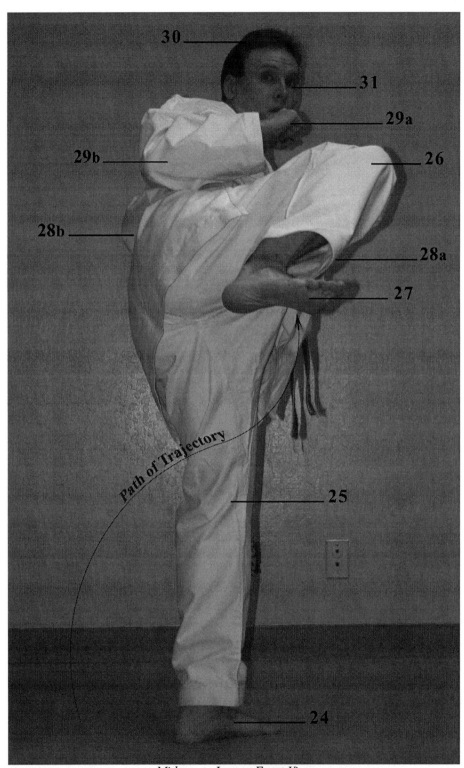

30 ——————

31

29a

29b ———————

26

28b ———————

28a

27

Path of Trajectory

25

24

Midway to Impact Front View

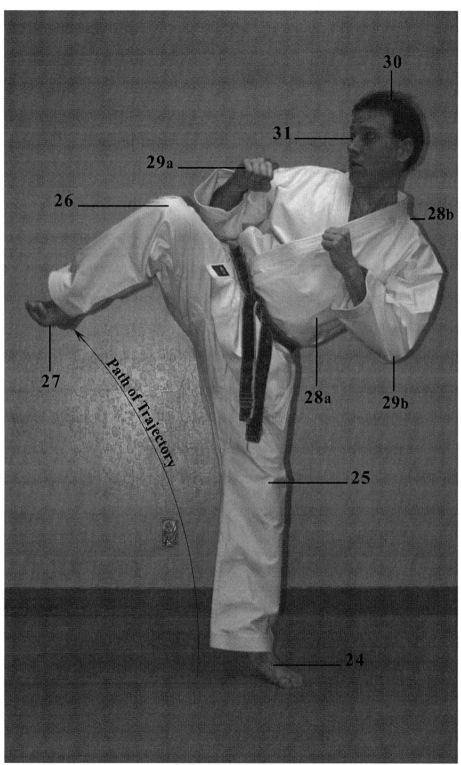

30

31

29a

26

28b

27

Path of Trajectory

28a

29b

25

24

Midway to Impact Side View

49

Impact:

Your base leg foot (32) should have now moved approximately 25-degrees counterclockwise by pivoting on the ball of your foot, while your base leg knee (33) remains slightly bent. In this position, the heel of your base leg foot will be closer to your opponent than your toes, and pointing at approximately a 45-degree angle to the left of your opponent. Your base leg foot (32) should also be pushing against the floor, while simultaneously gripping the floor with the entire foot. In other words, your entire foot should be in solid contact with the ground.

Impact
Foot Position

The toes on your kicking foot (35) remain flexed back toward your kicking leg knee in order to full expose the outside (knife) edge of your heel as the striking implement. Remember, your big toe will be the closest to your kicking knee, while your pinkie toe will be closer to your opponent. With the exception of the initial moment of "Impact," do not flex your kicking foot and toes to the point of having your foot and ankle too tight. It should be a relaxed tension or flexion. The outside (knife) edge of your heel on your kicking foot (35) should now be making contact with the appropriate vital or vulnerable point, in one of the selected target areas on your opponent. Remember that the contact time between your striking implement and the opponent's target area is minimal. Do not push the technique to the target area and then pull back. **Strike through the target and recoil!**

At the initial moment of impact, your kicking leg should be at 75% of full extension. There will be a slight bend in the kicking leg knee (34). The entire leg as well as the rest of the body will tighten up immediately upon impact with the target in order to add power to the kick. Then relax again, in order to facilitate a faster recoil. Your kicking leg knee should be pointed to the right of your opponent at a 90-degree angle in relation to the ground.

The front of your body (36a) and your back (36b), should still be facing in relatively the same positions that they were in during the "Coil" (20a-28a) and "Midway to Impact" positions (20b-28b). However, your upper body should now be leaning to your left, by bending over at the waist, at almost a 75-degree angle in relation to your body's previous upright position, and almost parallel with the ground. This position helps to facilitate an increased range of motion in order to properly execute the kick.

Your hands (37a) and elbows (37b), should still be up in relatively the same position as before in (29a) and (29b). Do not let them fly all over like a bird flapping its wings. Keep the elbows in to protect the rib cage and your hands up to protect your head. Your head (38) is still up with the chin tucked in behind the kicking leg shoulder. Your eyes (39) should still be looking over your kicking leg shoulder and focused on your opponent's chest.

Note: I cannot stress enough the importance of utilizing the proper relaxation and tension principles outlined in this book when executing this or any other kick, strike, or punch.

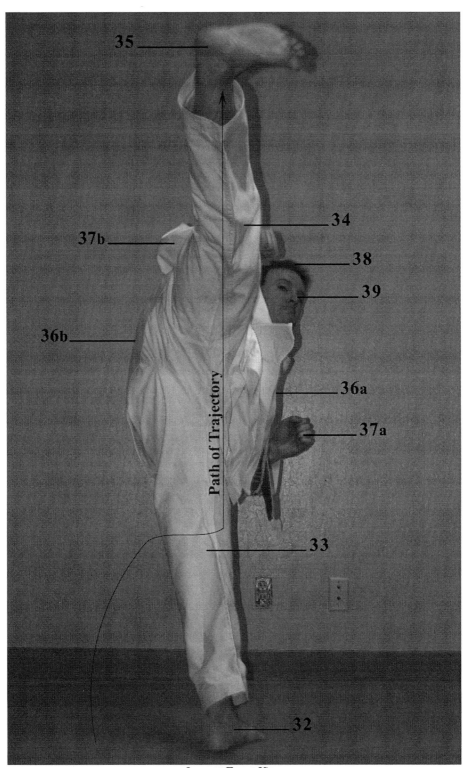

Impact Front View

Impact Side View

52

Recoil:

Your base leg foot (40) should now have moved approximately 45-degrees clockwise by pivoting on the ball of your base leg foot, so that the heel on your base leg foot is once again pointing at the 3 o'clock position, with your toes pointing at the 9 o'clock position. Your base leg will remain straight, with a slight bend in the knee (41).

Recoil
Foot Position

Your kicking leg foot (43) should return along exactly the same straight and even "Path of Trajectory" that it followed from the "Coil" position to "Impact," and should now be in exactly the same position that it was in during the "Coil" phase of this kick. Your kicking leg knee (42) should be directly in front of your body, and at least waist high, although it is even more effective when raised to lower chest height.

Your kicking foot (43) should be slightly in front of your base leg and as high above the base leg knee (41) as possible, while being tucked in close to your groin. The outside (knife) edge of your kicking foot should be pointed down towards the ground with your toes flexed back towards your kicking leg knee (42). Your big toe will be closest to your kicking knee, and your pinkie toe will be closer to the ground.

Even though you have already kicked your opponent, you may have to, or have the opportunity to, execute another Side Kick on your opponent before you can set your kicking foot (43) back down on the ground.

Too many martial artists are sacrificing a proper recoil in order to get their kicking foot back down on the ground faster. Although it is true to a certain extent that your kicking foot will get back down to the ground faster without recoiling, it is incorrect and can prove potentially harmful to the individual kicker. Proper technique should never be sacrificed for the sake of speed.

As you return to this position, your upper body should start to straighten up from its previous position. The front of your upper body (44a) should be facing at a 90-degree angle to your opponent's right, while your back (44b), which will obviously be facing in the opposite direction, will remain straight but not rigid. In this position, the kicking leg side of your body will remain closer to your opponent than your base leg side. Your hands (45a) and elbows (45b), are also in relatively the same position as in (37a) and (37b).

Your head (46), which is still facing toward your opponent, should remain looking directly over your kicking leg shoulder. Your eyes (47) should still be focused on your opponent, whether he is still standing, or lying on the ground.

Note: Can you easily grab something if it is within your reach and not moving? Can you easily grab something that is out of your reach and moving? Leave your kick "hanging" in the air and "posing," and your opponent will grab it. Recoil faster than you kicked, and he won't be able to grab it. If you make a mistake, your opponent will capitalize on it.

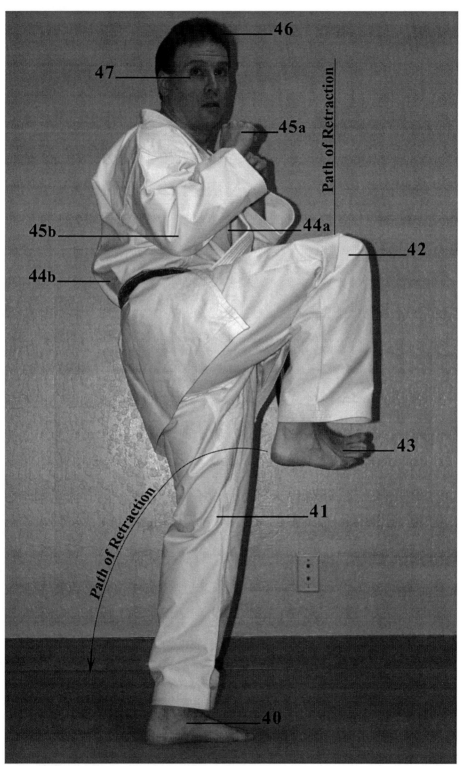

Recoil Position Front View

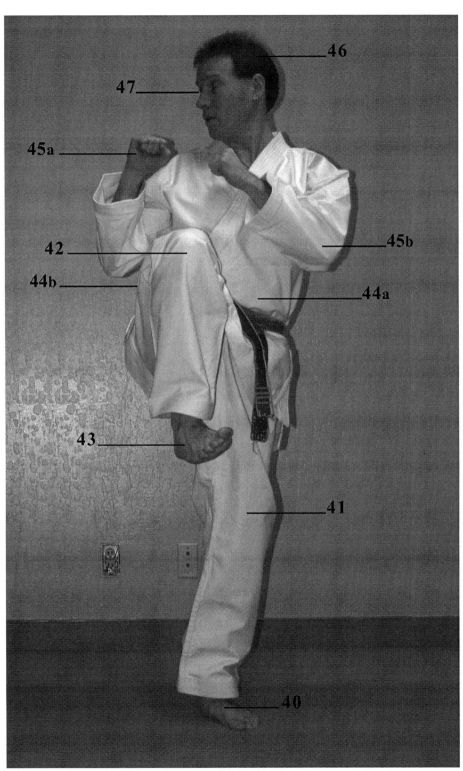

Recoil Position Side View

Lower Knee:

Although the initial lowering of your kicking leg knee (50) in preparation to "Return to Fighting Position" is rather simple to execute, its importance to the overall effectiveness of your kick should never be trivialized. This is done by first pivoting approximately 90-degrees clockwise on the ball of your base leg foot, so that the toes of your base leg foot (48) are now pointed directly at your opponent. Your base leg will continue to bear 100% of your body weight until your kicking foot returns back down on the ground during the "Return to Fighting Position" phase of the kick. Your base leg will remain straight with a slight bend in the base leg knee (49).

Lower Knee
Foot Position

Your kicking leg and kicking leg foot (51) will now return to the "Raise Knee" position. In this position, your kicking leg knee (50) will once again be up in front of you and toward the center of your body, until your knee is at least waist high. Your kicking foot (51) should remain directly underneath your upper leg so that the bottom of your heel is momentarily touching the inside of your base leg knee.

Your upper body, which should have also began turning in a clockwise direction, will now have the front of your upper body (52a) facing at approximately a 45-degree angle to your opponent's right. Your back (52b) should remain straight but not rigid. You should not be bent over at the waist at this time. The kicking leg side of your body will remain closer to your opponent than your base leg side.

Even though your hands (53a) and elbows (53b) have switched position throughout the execution of this kick, they should still be in relatively the same position as they were in your initial "Fighting Position." That is like a boxer, with the elbows tucked in to protect the ribs and your hands up to protect your head.

Your head (54) is still up and facing toward your opponent so that you are now looking over the right hand side of your chest, rather than your base leg shoulder. Your chin should still be tucked down close to your chest and behind your lead hand. Your eyes (55) if you have executed the kick properly, should still be in contact with your opponent, although they may not be focused on your opponent's chest if your opponent is lying on the ground. **Never take your eyes off of your opponent!**

Note: Balancing on one leg in order to execute a kick in a combat or self-defense situation, depends on a lot more than just knowing how to kick. The following are just a few of the conditions that must be factored into your decision on whether or not to kick. What is the surface area you are standing on? Is it flat and level? Is it slippery like tile or a hard wood floor? Is the area free of obstacles? What kind of shoes am I wearing? What time of day is it? What is the weather like? Am I wearing clothes that would restrict movement? Am I in an area with lots of room to move, or in a crowded area like a bar? Is this person by himself or with others? And most importantly, is this confrontation avoidable?

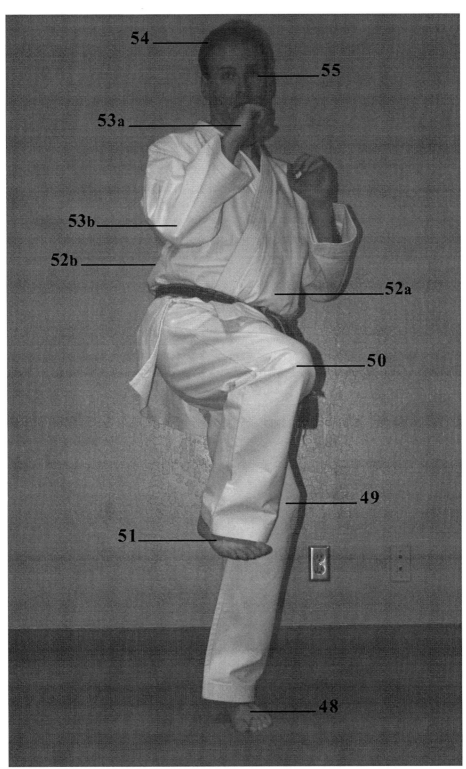

Lower Knee Front View

Lower Knee Side View

Return to Fighting Position #1:

After you have reached the "Lower Knee" position, sim- ply bring your kicking foot behind you and set it down, re- turning your kicking foot (56b) to its original starting posi- tion. Your head, shoulders, and hips will all come back around to your original fighting position before your kicking leg foot touches the ground. Your entire body should be upright and straight although not rigid throughout the entire return to your original fighting position.

Position #1

Once you return to "Fighting Position," your fighting stance should once again be approximately shoulder width apart with the toes of your front or lead foot (56a) pointed directly at your opponent. The heel of your lead foot (56a) should be in a direct line with the heel of your rear foot (56b). The toes of your back or rear foot (56b) should be pointed away from your body at a 45-degree angle. For example, if your right foot were in the rear position, then the toes of that foot would be pointed to the right at a 45-degree angle. If the left foot were in the rear position, then the toes of your left foot would be pointed to the left at a 45-degree angle.

Your weight should once again be distributed over the balls of both feet and not over the entire surface area of the feet. The weight distribution over your feet should be approximately 55% over the lead leg and 45% over the rear leg.

Your knees (57) should be slightly but not noticeably bent. The lead leg knee should be slightly bent over the lead leg foot in the direction of the toes. The same also holds true for the rear knee in the fact that it too should be slightly bent over the rear foot in the direction of the rear toes. The bending of the knees contributes to faster movement with the legs as they are not locked straight or rigid and have better mobility when slightly bent rather than straight.

Your body (58) is facing at a 45-degree angle to your opponent. Your hands (59a) and elbows (59b), should still be held up like a boxer's, that is with the lead hand held up at head level and away from your face about 8 to 12 inches (toward your oppo- nent). Your lead elbow should be tucked in along your side in order to protect your ribs and stomach area. Your rear hand is held up alongside your cheek with the palm of that hand facing toward your cheek. Your rear elbow is also tucked in along your side in order to protect your ribs and stomach area. Your back (60) should be straight but not rigid, and your lead shoulder should be raised up slightly in order to protect your chin.

Your head (61) is facing toward your opponent with the chin tucked down be- hind your upraised lead shoulder. Your eyes (62) should focus like a flashlight on the chest or center of your opponent whether he is still standing or not. At the same time, allow your peripheral vision to scan the rest of your opponent's body and therefore any movements that he might make. I cannot stress this enough, **do not** become fixated on a particular spot or point of focus on your opponent. This be- comes more of a hindrance than an asset when fighting.

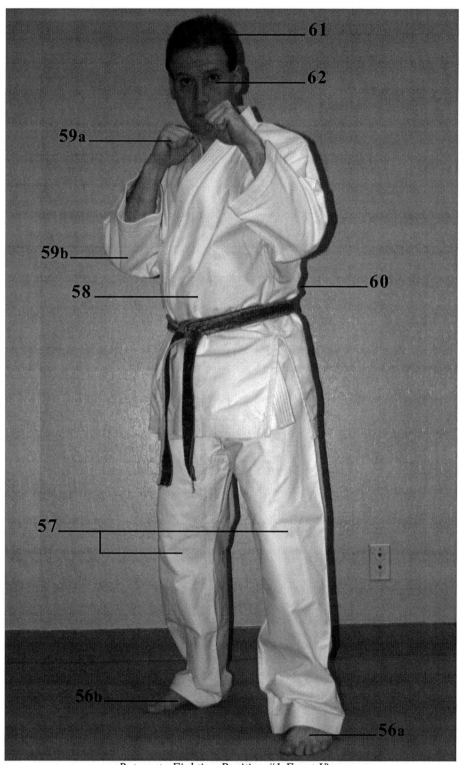

Return to Fighting Position #1 Front View

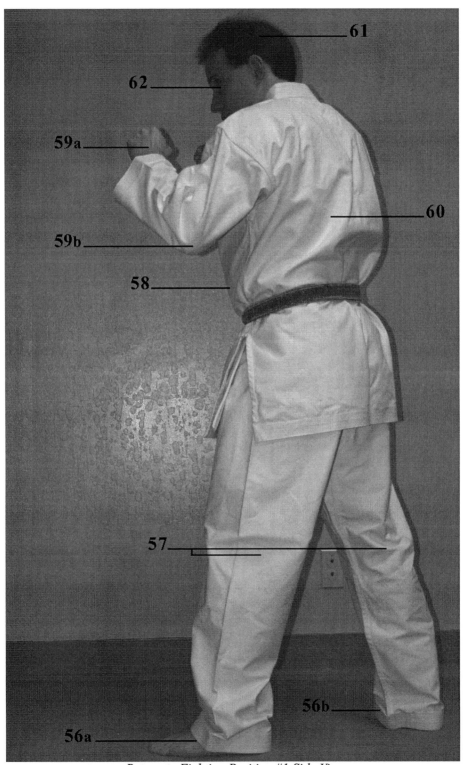

Return to Fighting Position #1 Side View

Return to Fighting Position #2:

After you have reached the "Lower Knee" position, simply leave your kicking foot in front of you. Instead of returning your kicking foot to its original starting position, set your kicking foot (63a) down in front of you and toward your opponent, with your kicking leg in the forward position, rather than in the rearward position. Remember that by stepping forward after this kick, you may be putting yourself in a more dangerous position because you are stepping in toward your opponent, which will put you closer to him. **Be extra cautious when executing this move.**

Position #2

Once you return to a "Fighting Position," your fighting stance should once again be approximately shoulder width apart (63a) with the toes of your front or lead foot pointed directly at your opponent. The heel of your lead foot should be in a direct line (63b) with the heel of your rear foot. The toes of your back or rear foot (63b) should be pointed away from your body at a 45-degree angle. For example, if your left foot were in the rear position, then the toes of that foot would be pointed to the left at a 45-degree angle. If the right foot were in the rear position, then the toes of your right foot would be pointed to the right at a 45-degree angle.

Your weight should once again be distributed over the balls of both feet and not over the entire surface are of the feet. The weight distribution over your feet should be approximately 55% over the lead leg and 45% over the rear leg.

Your knees (64) should be slightly but not noticeably bent. The lead leg knee should be slightly bent over the lead leg foot in the direction of the toes. The same also holds true for the rear knee in the fact that it too should be slightly bent over the rear foot in the direction of the rear toes. The bending of the knees contributes to faster movement with the legs as they are not locked straight or rigid and have better mobility when slightly bent rather than straight.

Your body (65) is facing at a 45-degree angle to your opponent. Your hands (66a) and elbows (66b), should still be held up like a boxer's, that is with the lead hand held up at head level and away from your face about 8 to 12 inches (toward your opponent). Your lead elbow should be tucked in along your side in order to protect your ribs and stomach area. Your rear hand is held up alongside your cheek with the palm of that hand facing toward your cheek. Your rear elbow is also tucked in along your side in order to protect your ribs and stomach area. Your back (67) should be straight but not rigid, and your lead shoulder should be raised up slightly in order to protect your chin.

Your head (68) is facing toward your opponent with the chin tucked down behind your upraised lead shoulder. Your eyes (69) should focus like a flashlight on the chest or center of your opponent whether he is still standing or lying on the ground. At the same time, allow your peripheral vision to scan the rest of your opponent's body, and therefore, any movements that he might make.

Return to Fighting Position #2 Front View

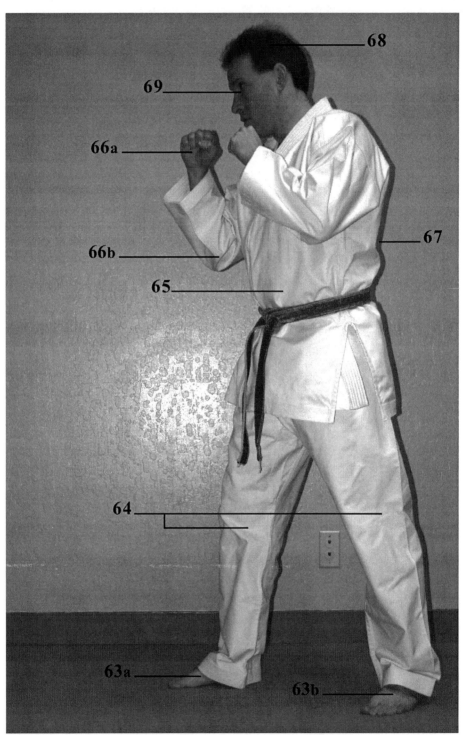

Return to Fighting Position #2 Side View

Pictorial Overview:

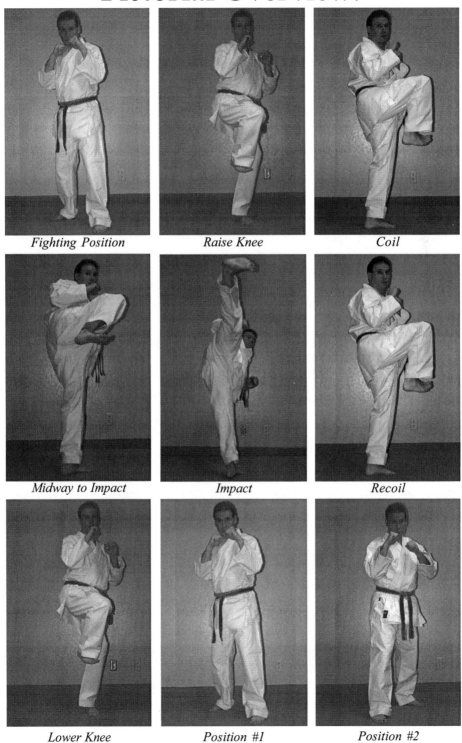

Fighting Position   Raise Knee   Coil

Midway to Impact   Impact   Recoil

Lower Knee   Position #1   Position #2

Variations of the Back Leg Side Kick

This chapter will explain in detail how to properly execute ten variations of the Back Leg Side Kick. Remember that all of these variations are derived from the primary kick, Back Leg Side Kick. Therefore, it is essential that you learn Back Leg Side Kick first before attempting any of these other variations.

To perhaps give you a better understanding of what I mean, let me use the comparison of building a house. Before you start building your house you are first going to need a set of blueprints, this would be the equivalent of the material presented in this book. Next you are going to need the proper materials to begin building with, this would be the equivalent of properly warming-up and stretching before you attempt to practice these kicks.

Next comes the hardest part for students to understand, now in order for your house to be stable, sturdy, and secure you must first have a very well built and strong foundation. The foundation of your house is made out of concrete, while the foundation of this particular type of kick is, the Back Leg Side Kick. Once you have a strong and proficient Back Leg Side Kick, then you can begin to build upon that with the many different variations of that kick. Just like you would build your frame, walls, ceilings, floors, and roof of your house.

If you don't take the time to first build a strong and stable foundation, your kicking skills along with your house, will not last and will collapse when the first strong storm or self-defense situation comes along.

As a general rule-of-thumb, every time you practice one of the variations of Back Leg Side Kick, you should practice Back Leg Side Kick itself at least ten times. I promise you that if you do this, all of your Side Kicks will steadily improve and become stronger.

Turning Side Kick

The Turning Side Kick is identical in execution to the Back Leg Side Kick, with one notable exception. A 180-degree semi-circular turning motion, which is initiated immediately prior to executing the kick, and can be followed by another 180-degree semi-circular turning motion, which would return you to your original starting position. This turning motion is used to either draw your opponent into you, or to confuse your opponent. It can also increase the power in this kick due to the added momentum of turning. The starting or fighting position for this kick is exactly the same at it was for Back Leg Side Kick, with your kicking leg in the rearward position rather than in the forward position. The actual turning motion prior to the execution of the kick, is performed by simply pivoting clockwise on the ball of your lead or base leg foot, while simultaneously turning and bringing your kicking leg and foot up into the proper "Coil" position. When executing the turning motion, be sure and move your base leg foot and kicking foot without initially moving your hips and upper body in order to avoid telegraphing the movement to your opponent. Your hips and upper body will begin to move as you start turning.

Fighting Position:

1. Your fighting position for this kick is exactly the same as it was for Back Leg Side Kick. With your kicking leg in the rearward position to begin with rather than in the forward position.

2. This stance is approximately shoulder width apart with the heel of your rear foot in a direct line with the heel of your front foot.

3. Your front or lead foot should be pointing directly at your opponent.

4. Your rear foot is angled toward the right at approximately a 45-degree angle. Your weight should be distributed evenly over the balls of both feet.

5. Your knees are slightly, but not noticeably bent. They should not be locked straight or rigid.

6. Your body should be facing at a 45-degree angle toward your opponent. This presents a smaller target area and also facilitates a faster turn, which allows you the opportunity to initiate a faster kick.

7. Your hands should be held up (like a boxers), with the elbows tucked in to protect the ribs and your hands up to protect your head. Your hands should remain as close to this position as possible throughout the entire kick.

8. Your head should be facing your opponent with your chin tucked down and protected by your lead shoulder.

9. Your eyes should be centered on your opponent's chest.

*Fighting Position
Foot Position*

Fighting Position Front View

Fighting Position Side View

67

Turning:

10. Turn 180-degrees clockwise by pivoting on the ball of your base leg foot so that your lead foot heel is now pointed directly at your opponent. While you are doing this, your rear foot is going to slide over approximately 8 inches while also turning 135-degrees clockwise so that the rear or kicking leg heel is also pointed directly at your opponent, while the toes of both feet are facing directly away from your opponent. Both knees are slightly, but not noticeably bent.

11. Your back should be straight and facing directly towards your opponent (at the 12 o'clock position), with the shoulder of your kicking leg slightly forward and toward your opponent.

12. Your hands and elbows should still be in relatively the same position as they were in the previous "Fighting Position."

13. Your head is turned so that you are looking over your kicking leg shoulder. Your chin is tucked down behind your kicking leg shoulder, and your eyes should still be centered on your opponent's chest.

*Turning
Foot Position*

Note: Your head should always turn first when executing any turning kick, so that you can maintain constant eye contact with your opponent.

Turning Front View

Turning Side View

Raise Knee:

14. Using the toes of your kicking foot, push off the floor and bring your kicking leg knee up directly in front of you. Your knee should be at least waist high, and your kicking foot should already be in the correct position to strike your opponent. In this position, your kicking knee should not be visible to your opponent.

15. As you raise your kicking knee, try not to move your hips and upper body in order to avoid telegraphing the movement to your opponent.

16. Although your hands have switched position, they should still be held up (like a boxer's), with the elbows tucked in to protect the ribs and your hands up to protect your head.

17. Your head should still be looking over your kicking leg shoulder, while your eyes remain in contact with your opponent throughout the entire kick.

Raise Knee Foot Position

Note: If you had an overhead view of the "Turning" portion of this technique, it would resemble a "smiley" face. The number 1, in the illustration on the right, represents the position your kicking foot is in prior to the turn. The number 2 represents the position of your kicking foot after completing the turn.

Raise Knee Front View

Raise Knee Side View

Coil:

18. Your base leg foot should now have moved approximately 90-degrees (clockwise) by pivoting on the ball of your foot.
19. Even though your body position has changed, your kicking leg knee should remain directly in front of your body, and at least waist high. While your kicking foot should be in front of and above your base leg knee.
20. Turn your body clockwise so that the kicking leg side of your body is now facing directly towards your opponent.
21. Your head should still be looking over your kicking shoulder, while your eyes remain in contact with your opponent.

Coil
Foot Position

Coil Position Front View

Coil Position Side View

Close Up:

19a. Your kicking leg foot is slightly in front of your base leg, and as high above the knee as possible, while being tucked in close to your groin. This gives you a tighter coil and helps keep your heel on a straight and even "Path of Trajectory."
19b. The outside (knife) edge of your kicking foot is pointed down towards the ground with your big toe closest to your kicking knee, and your pinkie toe closest to the ground. This helps maintain the proper foot position, and also makes the foot and ankle more rigid when kicking.
19c. Your kicking leg calf and hamstring muscles should make considerable contact with one another in the coil position.

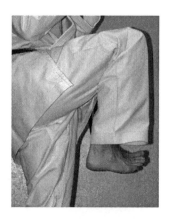

Close Up of Coil

70

Midway to Impact:

22. Your base leg foot should have moved approximately 20-degrees (counterclockwise) by pivoting on the ball of your foot, while your base leg knee remains slightly bent.

23. Your kicking leg knee should be pointed to the side, and in this position, be almost parallel with the ground. The heel on your kicking foot should follow a straight and even "Path of Trajectory" from the "Coil" position to "Impact."

Midway to Impact Foot Position

24. Your upper body should now start to lean over to your left at almost a 45-degree angle in relation to your body's previous upright position.

25. Your back should still be facing in the same direction as it was in the "Coil" position. That is facing at a 90-degree angle to your opponent's left. In this position, the kicking leg side of your body should be facing directly towards your opponent.

26. Although your body is now in the above position, your head should still be looking over your kicking leg shoulder, while your eyes remain in contact with your opponent.

Note: The optimum distance for initial impact with the target is at approximately 75% of full extension. If you strike the target at say 95% of full extension, the result is going to be a "surface strike," rather than a penetrating impact. If you strike the target at say 50% of full extension, the result is going to be little more than a hard push.

Midway to Impact Front View

Midway to Impact Side View

Impact:

27. Your base leg foot should now have moved approximately 25-degrees (counterclockwise) by pivoting on the ball of your foot, while the knee on your base leg remains slightly bent. In this position, the heel of your foot will be closer to your opponent than your toes and pointing at approximately a 45-degree angle to the left of your opponent.

Impact
Foot Position

28. Notice how your kicking foot, kicking leg (with knee slightly bent), hips, back, shoulders, and head are all in a straight line at the initial moment of "Impact." Also, notice how the outside edge of your kicking foot is extended and that the toes of the kicking foot are pulled back towards your knee. This helps insure that contact with the target is made with the outside (knife) edge of the heel.

29. Your upper body should now be leaning to your left at almost a 75-degree angle in relation to your body's previous upright position, and almost parallel with the ground. At the moment of impact, your entire body should tighten to add power to the kick as your foot continues to "strike through" the target.

30. Your head should still be up and looking over the kicking leg shoulder. Eye contact with your opponent is maintained at all times.

Note: If you are too slow on "Recoiling" your kicking leg, I guarantee you that your opponent will not be slow in grabbing it.

Impact Front View

Impact Side View

Recoil:

31. Your base leg foot should now have moved approximately 45-degrees (clockwise) by pivoting on the ball of your base leg foot. Returning it to the exact same position it was in during the "Coil" position.

32. Your kicking leg foot should return along exactly the same straight and even "Path of Trajectory" it followed from the "Coil" position to "Impact." Your kicking leg foot and knee should now be in the exact same position that they were in during the "Coil" position.

33. Your upper body should straighten up from the previous position you were in during the "Impact" phase of the kick. Your back is straight, but not rigid, and is still facing at a 90-degree angle to your opponent's left. In this position, the kicking leg side of your body should be facing directly towards your opponent.

34. Your head should have remained looking over your kicking leg shoulder. Your eyes are still in contact with your opponent, whether he is still standing, or lying on the ground.

Recoil
Foot Position

Note: Whether or not you are kicking to the body or head, the same principle of "striking through" the target applies. However, you must keep in mind that the head moves a lot easier than the body, is farther from the ground than the body, and generally speaking, it takes longer for a kick to get from the ground to the head, then from the ground to the body.

Recoil Position Front View

Recoil Position Side View

Lower Knee:

35. Your base leg foot should have moved approximately 90-degrees (clockwise), by pivoting on the ball of the foot. The toes of your base leg foot should now be pointing directly at your opponent.

36. Your kicking leg and foot will now return to the "Raise Knee" position, with your kicking leg knee up in front of you and at least waist high. Your kicking foot should have remained in the correct position to strike your opponent.

Lower Knee Foot Position

37. Your upper body, which should have also began turning in a clockwise direction, is now facing at approximately a 45-degree angle to your opponent's right. Your back remains straight, but not rigid. Although your hands have switched position throughout the kick, they should still be held up (like a boxer's), with the elbows tucked in to protect the ribs and your hands up to protect your head.

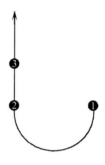

38. Your head should still be up and looking over your kicking leg shoulder. Your eyes are still in contact with your opponent, whether he is still standing, or lying on the ground.

Note: The overhead view of the "Path of Trajectory" of this kick from "Fighting Position" to "Impact," resembles a backwards J, when kicking with the right leg, and a regular J when kicking with the left leg. **(1)** The position your kicking foot is in prior to the turn. **(2)** The position of your kicking foot after completing the turn. **(3)** Midway to Impact.

Lower Knee Front View   *Lower Knee Side View*

Return to Fighting Position:

There are two ways that you can return to a fighting position from the "Lower Knee" position. They are as follows:

39a. After you have reached the "Lower Knee" position, simply bring your kicking foot behind you and set it down into a fighting position with your kicking leg behind you, rather than in front of you.

Position #1

39b. After you have reached the "Lower Knee" position, simply leave your kicking foot in front of you and set it down into a fighting position with your kicking leg in front of you, rather than behind you.

Position #2

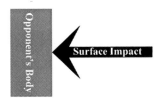

Note: As you can see in the illustrations presented above, you want to <u>STRIKE THROUGH</u> your opponent utilizing a penetrating impact, rather than utilizing a surface impact. Think of the striking implement of your kicking foot as a large caliber bullet being fired out of a high-powered rifle (your entire body), and going completely through the intended target.

75

Pictorial Overview:

Fighting Position

Turn

Raise Knee & Coil

Midway to Impact

Full Extension

Recoil

Lower Knee

Position #1

Position #2

Step-Behind Side Kick

The Step-Behind Side Kick is identical to the Front Leg Side Kick, with one notable exception. A stepping behind and forward motion is performed with your rear foot, prior to executing the kick. This step is used to close the distance with your opponent, and to increase the power in your kick. The actual stepping behind your lead foot with your rear foot prior to the execution of the kick is performed by stepping behind your lead foot while moving forward approximately 8 to 12 inches with your rear foot. When executing the stepping behind moving forward motion, be sure and move your rear foot and leg without initially moving your hips or upper body in order to avoid telegraphing the movement to your opponent. Your hips and upper body will begin to move after your rear foot has moved to its new position, not before.

Fighting Position:

1. Your fighting position for this kick is the exact same as it is for Spinning Side Kick. That is your kicking leg will be in the forward position to begin with rather than in the rear.
2. This stance is approximately shoulder width apart with the heel of your rear foot in a direct line with the heel of your front foot.
3. Your front or lead foot should be pointing directly at your opponent.
4. Your rear foot is angled towards the left at approximately a 45-degree angle. Your weight should be distributed evenly over the balls of both feet.
5. Your knees are slightly, but not noticeably bent. They should

Fighting Position
Foot Position

Fighting Position Front View

Step Behind

Fighting Position Side View

not be locked or rigid.

6. Your body should be facing at a 45-degree angle toward your opponent. This presents a smaller target area and also facilitates a faster step-behind, which allows you the opportunity to initiate a faster kick.

7. Your hands should be held up (like a boxer's), with the elbows tucked in to protect the ribs and your hands up to protect your head. Your hands should remain as close to this position as possible throughout the entire kick.

8. Your head should be facing your opponent with your chin tucked down and protected by your lead shoulder.

9. Your eyes should be centered on your opponents chest.

Step-Behind:

10. Keeping your upper body and hips as still as possible, step forward and behind the back of your lead leg foot with your rear leg foot.

11. When you place your rear foot back down on the ground, it should be approximately 8 to 12 inches in front of your lead foot, with the toes of your rear foot aligned with the center of your lead foot.

12. As soon as the ball of your rear foot touches the ground, begin to execute the kick.

13. Your eyes should still be centered on your opponent's chest.

Step-Behind Foot Position

Step Behind Front View   *Step Behind Side View*

Coil:

14. Your base leg foot should now have moved approximately 90-degrees (clockwise) by pivoting on the ball of your foot.

15. Even though your body position has changed, your kicking leg knee should remain directly in front of your body, and at least waist high. While your kicking foot should be in front of and above your base leg knee.

16. Turn your body clockwise so that the kicking leg side of your body is now facing directly towards your opponent.

17. Your head should still be looking over your kicking shoulder, while your eyes remain in contact with your opponent.

Coil
Foot Position

Coil Position Front View

Coil Position Side View

Close Up:

15a. Your kicking leg foot is slightly in front of your base leg, and as high above the knee as possible, while being tucked in close to your groin. This gives you a tighter coil and helps keep your heel on a straight and even "Path of Trajectory."

15b. The outside (knife) edge of your kicking foot is pointed down towards the ground with your big toe closest to your kicking knee, and your pinkie toe closest to the ground. This helps maintain the proper foot position, and also makes the foot and ankle more rigid when kicking.

15c. Your kicking leg calf and hamstring muscles should make considerable contact with one another in the coil position.

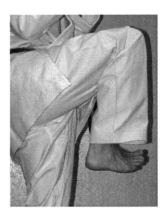

Close Up of Coil

Midway to Impact:

18. Your base leg foot should have moved approximately 20-degrees (counterclockwise) by pivoting on the ball of your foot, while your base leg knee remains slightly bent.

19. Your kicking leg knee should be pointed to the side, and in this position, be almost parallel with the ground. The heel on your kicking foot should follow a straight and even "Path of Trajectory" from the "Coil" position to "Impact."

Midway to Impact Foot Position

20. Your upper body should now start to lean over to your left at almost a 45-degree angle in relation to your body's previous upright position.

21. Your back should still be facing in the same direction as it was in the "Coil" position. That is facing at a 90-degree angle to your opponent's left. In this position, the kicking leg side of your body should be facing directly towards your opponent.

22. Although your body is now in the above position, your head should still be looking over your kicking leg shoulder, while your eyes remain in contact with your opponent.

Note: Utilize proper footwork prior to executing your kick in order to get the optimum kicking range between you and your opponent. If you are too far away, you will not hit your target. If you are too close, you will "jam" your own kick. Either one of these is ineffective and has the potential to leave you in a very dangerous position.

Midway to Impact Front View   *Midway to Impact Side View*

Impact:

23. Your base leg foot should now have moved approximately 25-degrees (counterclockwise) by pivoting on the ball of your foot, while the knee on your base leg remains slightly bent. In this position, the heel of your foot will be closer to your opponent than your toes and pointing at approximately a 45-degree angle to the left of your opponent.

*Impact
Foot Position*

24. Notice how your kicking foot, kicking leg (with knee slightly bent), hips, back, shoulders, and head are all in a straight line at the initial moment of "Impact." Also, notice how the outside edge of your kicking foot is extended and that the toes of the kicking foot are pulled back towards your knee. This helps insure that contact with the target is made with the outside (knife) edge of the heel.

25. Your upper body should now be leaning to your left at almost a 75-degree angle in relation to your body's previous upright position, and almost parallel with the ground. At the moment of impact, your entire body should tighten to add power to the kick as your foot continues to "strike through" the target.

26. Your head should still be up and looking over the kicking leg shoulder. Eye contact with your opponent is maintained at all times.

Note: Never hit your target, <u>STRIKE THROUGH</u> your target and retract or recoil immediately.

Impact Front View   *Impact Side View*

81

Recoil:

27. Your base leg foot should now have moved approximately 45-degrees (clockwise) by pivoting on the ball of your base leg foot. Returning it to the exact same position it was in during the "Coil" position.

28. Your kicking leg foot should return along exactly the same straight and even "Path of Trajectory" it followed from the "Coil" position to "Impact." Your kicking leg foot and knee should now be in the exact same position that they were in during the "Coil" position.

Recoil
Foot Position

29. Your upper body should straighten up from the previous position you were in during the "Impact" phase of the kick. Your back is straight, but not rigid, and is still facing at a 90-degree angle to your opponent's left. In this position, the kicking leg side of your body should be facing directly towards your opponent.

30. Your head should have remained looking over your kicking leg shoulder. Your eyes are still in contact with your opponent, whether he is still standing, or lying on the ground.

Note: Your kicking leg should be just as fast, if not faster, traveling from "Impact" to "Return to Fighting Position," than it is traveling from "Fighting Position" to "Impact."

Recoil Position Front View

Recoil Position Side View

Step Back Across:

31. Your kicking leg foot should return along the exact same path it followed from the "Step-Behind" position to the "Coil" position. Start by setting your kicking foot down in front of, and across your lead foot.

Step Back Across Foot Position

32. When you place your kicking foot back down on the ground, it should be approximately 8 to 12 inches behind your base leg foot, with the toes of your base leg foot aligned with the center of your kicking foot. As soon as the ball of your kicking foot touches the ground, begin to return to a fighting position.

33. Your upper body and back should still be in relatively the same position that they were in during the "Recoil" phase of this kick.

34. Your head should still be looking over your kicking leg shoulder, with your eyes in contact with your opponent, whether he is still standing, or lying on the ground.

Note: After you have become sufficiently proficient executing the kicks described in this book wearing gi pants and being barefoot, you will want to also start practicing them wearing your normal everyday clothes and shoes. There is a big difference between kicking in gi pants and barefoot, and kicking in everyday clothes and shoes.

Step Back Across Front View

Step Back Across Side View

Return to Fighting Position:

35. Pivoting 90-degrees (clockwise) on the ball of your kicking leg foot, step back with your base leg foot into your original fighting position.

36. Your upper body will return to facing at a 45-degree angle toward your opponent.

37. Your hands should still be held up (like a boxer's), with the elbows tucked in to protect the ribs and your hands up to protect your head. Your hands should have remained as close to this position as possible throughout the entire kick.

38. Your head should still be facing your opponent with your chin tucked down and protected by your lead shoulder.

38. Your eyes, as always, remain in contact with your opponent.

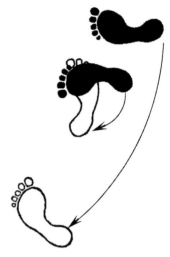

*Return to Fighting Position
Foot Position*

Note: **In order to generate the maximum amount of power possible when executing the Side Kick, you must adhere to the correct execution of movement throughout the entire kicking sequence. Just as in boxing, power must first be generated by the movement of the feet, legs, hips, body, and shoulders prior to "striking through" your target.**

Return to Fighting Position Front View

Return to Fighting Position Side View

Pictorial Overview:

Fighting Position

Step-Behind

Coil

Midway to Impact

Impact

Recoil

Step Back Across

Return to Fighting Position

Spinning Side Kick

The Spinning Side Kick is identical in execution to the Turning Side Kick, with one notable exception. A stepping forward motion, which is performed immediately prior to executing the kick. This step is used to close the distance with ones opponent, and when used properly, to misdirect or deceive your opponent in order to increase your chances of successfully executing the kick. It can also increase the power in this kick due to the added momentum obtained from stepping forward. The actual spinning motion of the rearward foot prior to execution of the kick is performed by simply stepping forward with the rear foot into another fighting position. Only now the kicking leg is in the rearward, rather than the forward position. When executing the step forward and turn, be sure and move your rear foot without initially moving your hips and upper body in order to avoid telegraphing the movement to your opponent. Your hips and upper body will begin to move as you set your foot back down on the ground.

Fighting Position:
1. Your fighting position for this kick is exactly the same as for Step-Behind Side Kick, with your kicking leg in the forward position to begin with rather than in the rear.
2. This stance is approximately shoulder width apart with the heel of your rear foot directly in line with the heel of your front foot.
3. Your front or lead foot should be pointed directly at your opponent.
4. Your rear foot is angled toward the left at approximately a 45-degree angle. Your weight should be distributed evenly

Fighting Position
Foot Position

Fighting Position Front View

Fighting Position Side View

over the balls of both feet.

5. Your knees are slightly, but not noticeably bent. They should not be locked straight or rigid.

6. Your body should be facing at a 45-degree angle towards your opponent. This presents a smaller target area and also facilitates a faster step-forward and turn, which allows you the opportunity to initiate a faster kick.

7. Your hands should be held up (like a boxer's), with the elbows tucked in to protect the ribs and your hands up to protect your head. Your hands should remain as close to this position as possible throughout the entire kick.

8. Your head should be facing your opponent with your chin tucked down and protected by your lead shoulder.

9. Your eyes should be centered on your opponent's chest.

Step Forward & Turn Back:

10. Take a step forward with your rear foot. And…

11. As you step forward with your rear leg, pivot on the ball of your base leg foot. This will have the effect of turning your back toward your opponent.

12. When you set your rear foot down, it should be not only in front of you, but also approximately 8 inches to the side. This allows for better balance and a more accurate kick. Your back should now be facing toward your opponent, and the heel of your now-base leg foot should also be pointed toward your opponent.

13. Your eyes should still be centered on your opponent's chest.

*Step Forward &
Turn Back
Foot Position*

Step Forward & Turn Front View

Step Forward & Turn Side View

87

Raise Knee:

14. Using the toes of your kicking foot, push off the floor and bring your kicking leg knee up directly in front of you. Your knee should be at least waist high, and your kicking foot should already be in the correct position to strike your opponent. In this position, your kicking knee should not be visible to your opponent.

15. As you raise your kicking knee, try not to move your hips and upper body in order to avoid telegraphing the movement to your opponent.

16. Although your hands have switched position, they should still be held up (like a boxer's), with the elbows tucked in to protect the ribs and your hands up to protect your head.

17. Your head should still be looking over your kicking leg shoulder, while your eyes remain in contact with your opponent throughout the entire kick.

Raise Knee
Foot Position

Note: Although a separate ten volume set of books focusing on the combat and tournament applications of each of the ten primary kicks is currently being written, I would like to have you consider the following, "Couldn't the very motion of the "step forward" also be a Roundhouse Kick followed by a Turning Side Kick?"

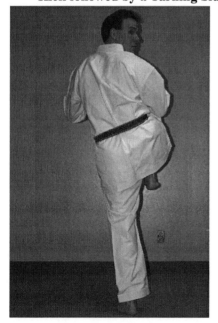

Raise Knee Front View   *Raise Knee Side View*

Coil:

18. Your base leg foot should now have moved approximately 90-degrees (clockwise) by pivoting on the ball of your foot.
19. Even though your body position has changed, your kicking leg knee should remain directly in front of your body, and at least waist high. While your kicking foot should be in front of and above your base leg knee.
20. Turn your body clockwise so that the kicking leg side of your body is now facing directly towards your opponent.
21. Your head should still be looking over your kicking shoulder, while your eyes remain in contact with your opponent.

Coil
Foot Position

Coil Position Front View

Coil Position Side View

Close Up:

19a. Your kicking leg foot is slightly in front of your base leg, and as high above the knee as possible, while being tucked in close to your groin. This gives you a tighter coil and helps keep your heel on a straight and even "Path of Trajectory."
19b. The outside (knife) edge of your kicking foot is pointed down towards the ground with your big toe closest to your kicking knee, and your pinkie toe closest to the ground. This helps maintain the proper foot position, and also makes the foot and ankle more rigid when kicking.
19c. Your kicking leg calf and hamstring muscles should make considerable contact with one another in the coil position.

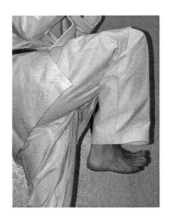

Close Up of Coil

Midway to Impact:

22. Your base leg foot should have moved approximately 20-degrees (counterclockwise) by pivoting on the ball of your foot, while your base leg knee remains slightly bent.

23. Your kicking leg knee should be pointed to the side, and in this position, be almost parallel with the ground. The heel on your kicking foot should follow a straight and even "Path of Trajectory" from the "Coil" position to "Impact."

Midway to Impact Foot Position

24. Your upper body should now start to lean over to your left at almost a 45-degree angle in relation to your body's previous upright position.

25. Your back should still be facing in the same direction as it was in the "Coil" position. That is facing at a 90-degree angle to your opponent's left. In this position, the kicking leg side of your body should be facing directly towards your opponent.

26. Although your body is now in the above position, your head should still be looking over your kicking leg shoulder, while your eyes remain in contact with your opponent.

Note: Another mistake that is quite common with martial artists, is to kick too high and go over their opponent's head. Don't kick over your opponent's head, <u>kick through your opponent's head!</u>

Midway to Impact Front View   *Midway to Impact Side View*

90

Impact:

27. Your base leg foot should now have moved approximately 25-degrees (counterclockwise) by pivoting on the ball of your foot, while the knee on your base leg remains slightly bent. In this position, the heel of your foot will be closer to your opponent than your toes and pointing at approximately a 45-degree angle to the left of your opponent.

*Impact
Foot Position*

28. Notice how your kicking foot, kicking leg (with knee slightly bent), hips, back, shoulders, and head are all in a straight line at the initial moment of "Impact." Also, notice how the outside edge of your kicking foot is extended and that the toes of the kicking foot are pulled back towards your knee. This helps insure that contact with the target is made with the outside (knife) edge of the heel.

29. Your upper body should now be leaning to your left at almost a 75-degree angle in relation to your body's previous upright position, and almost parallel with the ground. At the moment of impact, your entire body should tighten to add power to the kick as your foot continues to "strike through" the target.

30. Your head should still be up and looking over the kicking leg shoulder. Eye contact with your opponent is maintained at all times.

Note: If you want to learn how to improve your strategic thinking, learn not only how to play the game of chess, but also how to study it.

Impact Front View   *Impact Side View*

Recoil:

31. Your base leg foot should now have moved approximately 45-degrees (clockwise) by pivoting on the ball of your base leg foot. Returning it to the exact same position it was in during the "Coil" position.

*Recoil
Foot Position*

32. Your kicking leg foot should return along exactly the same straight and even "Path of Trajectory" it followed from the "Coil" position to "Impact." Your kicking leg foot and knee should now be in the exact same position that they were in during the "Coil" position.

33. Your upper body should straighten up from the previous position you were in during the "Impact" phase of the kick. Your back is straight, but not rigid, and is still facing at a 90-degree angle to your opponent's left. In this position, the kicking leg side of your body should be facing directly towards your opponent.

34. Your head should have remained looking over your kicking leg shoulder. Your eyes are still in contact with your opponent, whether he is still standing, or lying on the ground.

Note: Although I have broken down all of the kicks in this book into various steps, you must remember that eventually you will be executing these kicks without thought in one fluid motion while adhering to every principle and technique described in this book in order to maximize the effectiveness of your kick.

Recoil Position Front View   *Recoil Position Side View*

Lower Knee:

35. Your base leg foot should have moved approximately 90-degrees (clockwise), by pivoting on the ball of the foot. The toes of your base leg foot should now be pointing directly at your opponent.

36. Your kicking leg and foot will now return to the "Raise Knee" position, with your kicking leg knee up in front of you and at least waist high. Your kicking foot should have remained in the correct position to strike your opponent.

*Lower Knee
Foot Position*

37. Your upper body, which should have also began turning in a clockwise direction, is now facing at approximately a 45-degree angle to your opponent's right. Your back remains straight, but not rigid. Although your hands have switched position throughout the kick, they should still be held up (like a boxer's), with the elbows tucked in to protect the ribs and your hands up to protect your head.

38. Your head should still be up and looking over your kicking leg shoulder. Your eyes are still in contact with your opponent, whether he is still standing, or lying on the ground.

Note: As a general rule-of-thumb, your initial impact point is at the surface of the target area (vital/vulnerable point) in which you intend to <u>STRIKE THROUGH</u>. Your impact continues <u>THROUGH</u> the body or head, and ends outside the body on the opposite side. Remember, <u>DO NOT PUSH</u> your opponent, <u>STRIKE THROUGH</u> your opponent.

Lower Knee Front View

Lower Knee Side View

Return to Fighting Position:

There are two ways that you can return to a fighting position from the "Lower Knee" position. They are as follows:

39a. After you have reached the "Lower Knee" position, simply bring your kicking foot behind you and set it down into a fighting position with your kicking leg behind you, rather than in front of you.

Position #1

39b. After you have reached the "Lower Knee" position, simply leave your kicking foot in front of you and set it down into a fighting position with your kicking leg in front of you, rather than behind you.

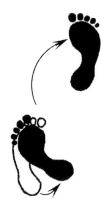

Position #2

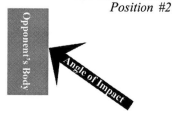

Note: As you can see in the illustrations presented above, the optimum angle for impact in relation to your opponent's body is a 90-degree angle. Therefore, the further away you are from a 90-degree angle, the less effective your kick is going to be. As you look at the illustrations above, imagine that you have not only an overhead view, but also a side view of your opponent's body. The black arrows are Side Kicks delivered to your opponent's solar plexus. Which one is going to be more effective, the one on the left? Or the one on the right?

94

Pictorial Overview:

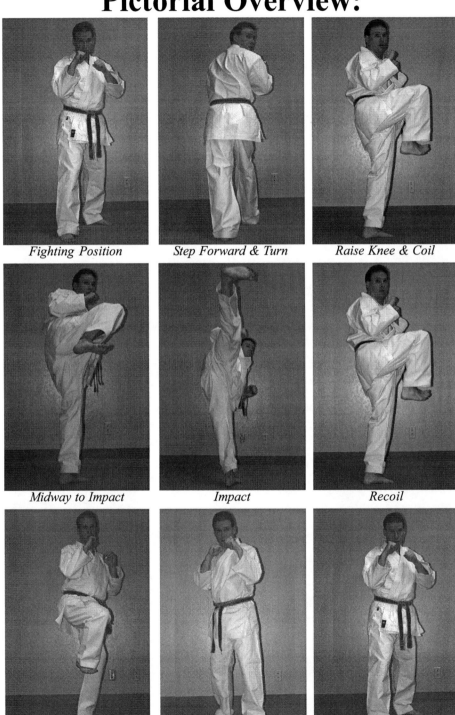

Fighting Position   Step Forward & Turn   Raise Knee & Coil

Midway to Impact   Impact   Recoil

Lower Knee   Position #1   Position #2

Hop/Slide Forward Side Kick

The Hopping/Sliding Forward Side Kick is identical in execution to the Back Leg Side Kick, with one notable exception. A hopping/sliding forward motion, which is performed immediately prior to executing the kick. This motion is used to close the distance between you and your opponent. It can also increase the power in this kick due to the added momentum of hopping/sliding forward. The actual hop or slide motion is performed by both feet simultaneously moving forward keeping the same distance between them. The hop or slide can be anywhere from a few inches up to 18 inches. Keep your hips and upper body as still as possible throughout the initial hop or slide forward in order to avoid telegraphing the move to your opponent.

Fighting Position:

1. Your fighting position for this kick is exactly the same as it was for Back Leg Side Kick. With your kicking leg in the rearward position to begin with, rather than in the forward position.
2. This stance is approximately shoulder width apart with the heel of your rear foot in a direct line with the heel of your front foot.
3. Your front or lead foot should be pointing directly at your opponent.
4. Your rear foot is angled toward the right at approximately a 45-degree angle. Your weight should be distributed evenly over the balls of both feet.
5. Your knees are slightly, but not noticeably bent. They should not be locked straight or rigid.
6. Your body should be facing at a 45-degree angle toward your opponent. This presents a smaller target area and

Fighting Position Foot Position

Fighting Position Front View

Fighting Position Side View

also facilitates a faster hop/slide forward, which allows you the opportunity to initiate a faster kick.

7. Your hands should be held up (like a boxers), with the elbows tucked in to protect the ribs and your hands up to protect your head. Your hands should remain as close to this position as possible throughout the entire kick.

8. Your head should be facing your opponent with your chin tucked down and protected by your lead shoulder.

9. Your eyes should be centered on your opponent's chest.

Hop/Slide Forward & Raise Knee:

10. Moving on the balls of your feet, move both feet forward approximately 3 to 18 inches, utilizing a hopping/sliding motion. As you are completing the hop/slide forward, you will begin to execute the kick.

11. Using the toes of your kicking foot, push off the floor and bring your kicking leg knee up directly in front of you and to the center. Your knee should be at least waist high, and your kicking foot should already be in the correct position to strike your opponent.

12. As your bring your kicking leg up, your upper body should now be facing at a slight angle toward your opponent. In this position, the kicking leg side of your body should be closer to your opponent than your base leg side. Your back will remain straight but not rigid.

13. Your head is up and facing towards your opponent, while your eyes remain in contact with your opponent throughout the entire kick.

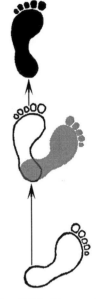

Hop/Slide Forward
& Raise Knee
Foot Position

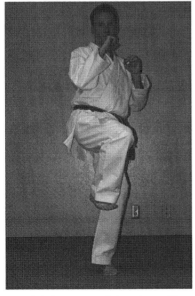

Hop/Slide Forward &... Front View

Hop/Slide Forward &... Side View

97

Coil:

14. Your base leg foot should have moved approximately 90-degrees (counterclockwise) by pivoting on the ball of your foot.

15. Even though your body position has changed, your kicking leg knee should remain directly in front of your body, and at least waist high. While your kicking foot should be in front of and above your base leg knee.

16. Turn your body counterclockwise so that the kicking leg side of your body is now facing directly towards your opponent.

17. Your head should still be looking over your kicking shoulder, while your eyes remain in contact with your opponent.

Coil Foot Position

Coil Position Front View

Coil Position Side View

Close Up:

15a. Your kicking leg foot is slightly in front of your base leg, and as high above the knee as possible, while being tucked in close to your groin. This gives you a tighter coil and helps keep your heel on a straight and even "Path of Trajectory."

15b. The outside (knife) edge of your kicking foot is pointed down towards the ground with your big toe closest to your kicking knee, and your pinkie toe closest to the ground. This helps maintain the proper foot position, and also makes the foot and ankle more rigid when kicking.

15c. Your kicking leg calf and hamstring muscles should make considerable contact with one another in the coil position.

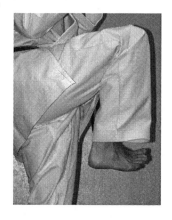

Close Up of Coil

Midway to Impact:

18. Your base leg foot should have moved approximately 20-degrees (counterclockwise) by pivoting on the ball of your foot, while your base leg knee remains slightly bent.

19. Your kicking leg knee should be pointed to the side, and in this position, be almost parallel with the ground. The heel on your kicking foot should follow a straight and even "Path of Trajectory" from the "Coil" position to "Impact."

Midway to Impact Foot Position

20. Your upper body should now start to lean over to your left at almost a 45-degree angle in relation to your body's previous upright position.

21. Your back should still be facing in the same direction as it was in the "Coil" position. That is facing at a 90-degree angle to your opponent's left. In this position, the kicking leg side of your body should be facing directly towards your opponent.

22. Although your body is now in the above position, your head should still be looking over your kicking leg shoulder, while your eyes remain in contact with your opponent.

Note: The available vital/vulnerable points that are open to attack is going to be determined by your opponent. However, you can create your own openings on your opponent not only by setting him up with various attack strategies (like a boxer utilizing the jab to set up a right cross or hook), but also by correctly utilizing deception prior to, and during your attack.

Midway to Impact Front View

Midway to Impact Side View

Impact:

23. Your base leg foot should now have moved approximately 25-degrees (counterclockwise) by pivoting on the ball of your foot, while the knee on your base leg remains slightly bent. In this position, the heel of your foot will be closer to your opponent than your toes and pointing at approximately a 45-degree angle to the left of your opponent.

*Impact
Foot Position*

24. Notice how your kicking foot, kicking leg (with knee slightly bent), hips, back, shoulders, and head are all in a straight line at the initial moment of "Impact." Also, notice how the outside edge of your kicking foot is extended and that the toes of the kicking foot are pulled back towards your knee. This helps insure that contact with the target is made with the outside (knife) edge of the heel.

25. Your upper body should now be leaning to your left at almost a 75-degree angle in relation to your body's previous upright position, and almost parallel with the ground. At the moment of impact, your entire body should tighten to add power to the kick as your foot continues to "strike through" the target.

26. Your head should still be up and looking over the kicking leg shoulder. Eye contact with your opponent is maintained at all times.

Note: For optimum results upon impact, your must use a combination of proper technique, along with and explosive combination of speed and strength.

Impact Front View

Impact Side View

Recoil:

27. Your base leg foot should now have moved approximately 45-degrees (clockwise) by pivoting on the ball of your base leg foot. Returning it to the exact same position it was in during the "Coil" position.

28. Your kicking leg foot should return along exactly the same straight and even "Path of Trajectory" it followed from the "Coil" position to "Impact." Your kicking leg foot and knee should now be in the exact same position that they were in during the "Coil" position.

29. Your upper body should straighten up from the previous position you were in during the "Impact" phase of the kick. Your back is straight, but not rigid, and is still facing at a 90-degree angle to your opponent's left. In this position, the kicking leg side of your body should be facing directly towards your opponent.

30. Your head should have remained looking over your kicking leg shoulder. Your eyes are still in contact with your opponent, whether he is still standing, or lying on the ground.

Recoil
Foot Position

Note: The ability to effectively and efficiently utilize high section kicks depends primarily on the following four factors. A: Your expertise in kicking. B: Your overall flexibility and physical condition. C: Your environment at the time. D: Your opponent.

Recoil Position Front View

Recoil Position Side View

Lower Knee:

31. Your base leg foot should have moved approximately 90-degrees (clockwise), by pivoting on the ball of the foot. The toes of your base leg foot should now be pointing directly at your opponent.

Lower Knee Foot Position

32. Your kicking leg and foot will now return to the "Raise Knee" position, with your kicking leg knee up in front of you and at least waist high. Your kicking foot should have remained in the correct position to strike your opponent.

33. Your upper body, which should have also began turning in a clockwise direction, is now facing at approximately a 45-degree angle to your opponent's right. Your back remains straight, but not rigid. Although your hands have switched position throughout the kick, they should still be held up (like a boxer's), with the elbows tucked in to protect the ribs and your hands up to protect your head.

34. Your head should still be up and looking over your kicking leg shoulder. Your eyes are still in contact with your opponent, whether he is still standing, or lying on the ground.

Note: If you leave your kicking foot "hanging" in the air after "striking through" your target, you have not only executed the kick improperly, but you have also left yourself in a very vulnerable position. One that your opponent may very easily exploit to his advantage.

Lower Knee Front View

Lower Knee Side View

Return to Fighting Position:

There are two ways that you can return to a fighting position from the "Lower Knee" position. They are as follows:

Position #1

35a. After you have reached the "Lower Knee" position, simply bring your kicking foot behind you and set it down into a fighting position with your kicking leg behind you, rather than in front of you.

35b. After you have reached the "Lower Knee" position, simply leave your kicking foot in front of you and set it down into a fighting position with your kicking leg in front of you, rather than behind you.

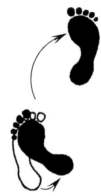

Position #2

Note: Once you become proficient executing this kick, you will want to strike your target at the exact same time that your base leg foot ends its hop/ slide forward. Remember that all of these kicks should eventually be executed in one fluid motion. However, one must first learn how to ex- ecute each stage of the kick correctly before putting it all together. TAKE YOUR TIME!

Pictorial Overview:

Fighting Position   Hop/Slide Forward &...   Coil

Midway to Impact   Impact   Recoil

Lower Knee   Position #1   Position #2

Hop/Slide Backward Side Kick

The Hopping/Sliding Backward Side Kick is identical in execution to the Back Leg Side Kick, with one notable exception. A hopping/sliding backward motion, which is performed immediately prior to executing the kick. This hopping/sliding backward motion is used to draw your opponent into you, or to avoid an attack. It can also increase the power in this kick due to the added momentum of hopping/sliding backward. The actual hop or slide motion is performed by both feet simultaneously moving backward keeping the same distance between them. The hop or slide can be anywhere from a few inches up to 18 inches. Keep your hips and upper body as still as possible throughout the initial hop or slide backward in order to avoid telegraphing the move to your opponent.

Fighting Position:

1. Your fighting position for this kick is exactly the same as it was for Back Leg Side Kick. With your kicking leg in the rearward position to begin with, rather than in the forward position.

2. This stance is approximately shoulder width apart with the heel of your rear foot in a direct line with the heel of your front foot.

3. Your front or lead foot should be pointing directly at your opponent.

4. Your rear foot is angled toward the right at approximately a 45-degree angle. Your weight should be distributed evenly over the balls of both feet.

5. Your knees are slightly, but not noticeably bent. They should not be locked straight or rigid.

6. Your body should be facing at a 45-degree angle toward

Fighting Position
Foot Position

Fighting Position Front View

Hop/Slide
Backward

Fighting Position Side View

your opponent. This presents a smaller target area and also facilitates a faster hop/slide backward, which allows you the opportunity to initiate a faster kick.

7. Your hands should be held up (like a boxers), with the elbows tucked in to protect the ribs and your hands up to protect your head. Your hands should remain as close to this position as possible throughout the entire kick.

8. Your head should be facing your opponent with your chin tucked down and protected by your lead shoulder.

9. Your eyes should be centered on your opponent's chest.

Hop/Slide Backward & Raise Knee:

10. Moving on the balls of your feet, move both feet backward approximately 3 to 18 inches, utilizing a hopping/sliding motion. As you are completing the hop/slide backward, you will begin to execute the kick.

11. Using the toes of your kicking foot, push off the floor and bring your kicking leg knee up directly in front of you and to the center. Your knee should be at least waist high, and your kicking foot should already be in the correct position to strike your opponent.

12. As your bring your kicking leg up, your upper body should now be facing at a slight angle toward your opponent. In this position, the kicking leg side of your body should be closer to your opponent than your base leg side. Your back will remain straight but not rigid

13. Your head is up and facing towards your opponent, while your eyes remain in contact with your opponent throughout the entire kick.

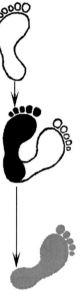

*Hop/Slide Backward
& Raise Knee
Foot Position*

Hop/Slide Backward &... Front View

Hop/Slide Backward &... Back View

106

Coil:

14. Your base leg foot should have moved approximately 90-degrees (counterclockwise) by pivoting on the ball of your foot.

15. Even though your body position has changed, your kicking leg knee should remain directly in front of your body, and at least waist high. While your kicking foot should be in front of and above your base leg knee.

16. Turn your body counterclockwise so that the kicking leg side of your body is now facing directly towards your opponent.

Coil
Foot Position

17. Your head should still be looking over your kicking shoulder, while your eyes remain in contact with your opponent.

Coil Position Front View

Coil Position Side View

Close Up:

15a. Your kicking leg foot is slightly in front of your base leg, and as high above the knee as possible, while being tucked in close to your groin. This gives you a tighter coil and helps keep your heel on a straight and even "Path of Trajectory."

15b. The outside (knife) edge of your kicking foot is pointed down towards the ground with your big toe closest to your kicking knee, and your pinkie toe closest to the ground. This helps maintain the proper foot position, and also makes the foot and ankle more rigid when kicking.

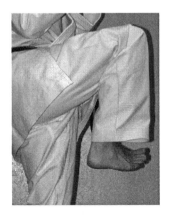

15c. Your kicking leg calf and hamstring muscles should make considerable contact with one another in the coil position.

Close Up of Coil

Midway to Impact:

18. Your base leg foot should have moved approximately 20-degrees (counterclockwise) by pivoting on the ball of your foot, while your base leg knee remains slightly bent.

19. Your kicking leg knee should be pointed to the side, and in this position, be almost parallel with the ground. The heel on your kicking foot should follow a straight and even "Path of Trajectory" from the "Coil" position to "Impact."

Midway to Impact
Foot Position

20. Your upper body should now start to lean over to your left at almost a 45-degree angle in relation to your body's previous upright position.

21. Your back should still be facing in the same direction as it was in the "Coil" position. That is facing at a 90-degree angle to your opponent's left. In this position, the kicking leg side of your body should be facing directly towards your opponent.

22. Although your body is now in the above position, your head should still be looking over your kicking leg shoulder, while your eyes remain in contact with your opponent.

Note: The head, which can easily be compared to the ever popular "bobblehead" dolls, makes for a difficult target with a kick due to the ease in which the head can "bob and weave" like a boxer in order to avoid being hit.

Midway to Impact Front View

Midway to Impact Side View

Impact:

23. Your base leg foot should now have moved approximately 25-degrees (counterclockwise) by pivoting on the ball of your foot, while the knee on your base leg remains slightly bent. In this position, the heel of your foot will be closer to your opponent than your toes and pointing at approximately a 45-degree angle to the left of your opponent.

Impact
Foot Position

24. Notice how your kicking foot, kicking leg (with knee slightly bent), hips, back, shoulders, and head are all in a straight line at the initial moment of "Impact." Also, notice how the outside edge of your kicking foot is extended and that the toes of the kicking foot are pulled back towards your knee. This helps insure that contact with the target is made with the outside (knife) edge of the heel.

25. Your upper body should now be leaning to your left at almost a 75-degree angle in relation to your body's previous upright position, and almost parallel with the ground. At the moment of impact, your entire body should tighten to add power to the kick as your foot continues to "strike through" the target.

26. Your head should still be up and looking over the kicking leg shoulder. Eye contact with your opponent is maintained at all times.

Note: Look closely at the photographs below, see how vulnerable you are in this position. Constantly strive to kick faster than you can blink!

Impact Front View

Impact Side View

109

Recoil:

27. Your base leg foot should now have moved approximately 45-degrees (clockwise) by pivoting on the ball of your base leg foot. Returning it to the exact same position it was in during the "Coil" position.

28. Your kicking leg foot should return along exactly the same straight and even "Path of Trajectory" it followed from the "Coil" position to "Impact." Your kicking leg foot and knee should now be in the exact same position that they were in during the "Coil" position.

29. Your upper body should straighten up from the previous position you were in during the "Impact" phase of the kick. Your back is straight, but not rigid, and is still facing at a 90-degree angle to your opponent's left. In this position, the kicking leg side of your body should be facing directly towards your opponent.

30. Your head should have remained looking over your kicking leg shoulder. Your eyes are still in contact with your opponent, whether he is still standing, or lying on the ground.

Recoil
Foot Position

Note: Would you hammer a nail into a piece of wood with a saw? Would you cut a board with a hammer? Remember to use the correct tool for each particular situation. Kicking may be effective in one situation, but ineffective in another. A Side Kick may be the correct kick to use in one kicking situation, but totally ineffective in another.

Recoil Position Front View

Recoil Position Side View

110

Lower Knee:

31. Your base leg foot should have moved approximately 90-degrees (clockwise), by pivoting on the ball of the foot. The toes of your base leg foot should now be pointing directly at your opponent.

32. Your kicking leg and foot will now return to the "Raise Knee" position, with your kicking leg knee up in front of you and at least waist high. Your kicking foot should have remained in the correct position to strike your opponent.

*Lower Knee
Foot Position*

33. Your upper body, which should have also began turning in a clockwise direction, is now facing at approximately a 45-degree angle to your opponent's right. Your back remains straight, but not rigid. Although your hands have switched position throughout the kick, they should still be held up (like a boxer's), with the elbows tucked in to protect the ribs and your hands up to protect your head.

34. Your head should still be up and looking over your kicking leg shoulder. Your eyes are still in contact with your opponent, whether he is still standing, or lying on the ground.

Note: Although this book details only one of the ten primary kicks and ten of its main variations. You must remember that there are nine more primary kicks, and their variations. Kicking is only one aspect of becoming a complete and effective fighter. One Should also study and practice hand and elbow techniques, throwing, grappling, and joint techniques.

Lower Knee Front View

Lower Knee Side View

Return to Fighting Position:

There are two ways that you can return to a fighting position from the "Lower Knee" position. They are as follows:

35a. After you have reached the "Lower Knee" position, simply bring your kicking foot behind you and set it down into a fighting position with your kicking leg behind you, rather than in front of you.

Position #1

35b. After you have reached the "Lower Knee" position, simply leave your kicking foot in front of you and set it down into a fighting position with your kicking leg in front of you, rather than behind you.

Position #2

Note: Unlike the Hop/Slide Forward Side Kick, the hopping or sliding motion of the Hop/Slide Backward Side Kick will initially remain separate from the actual kick itself. This is primarily due to the fact that your momentum, which is initially moving backwards, has to stop altogether in order for you to reverse direction and execute the kick. However, as you become more proficient at executing both portions of this kick independently from one another, you will eventually combine them into one fluid motion. You will find that as the ball of your back foot touches the ground, you will "push off" with that foot in order to immediately change directions and begin initiating the kick. While at the same time your front foot plants itself firmly in front. This is not easy to do and takes time, patience, and lots of correct practice.

Pictorial Overview:

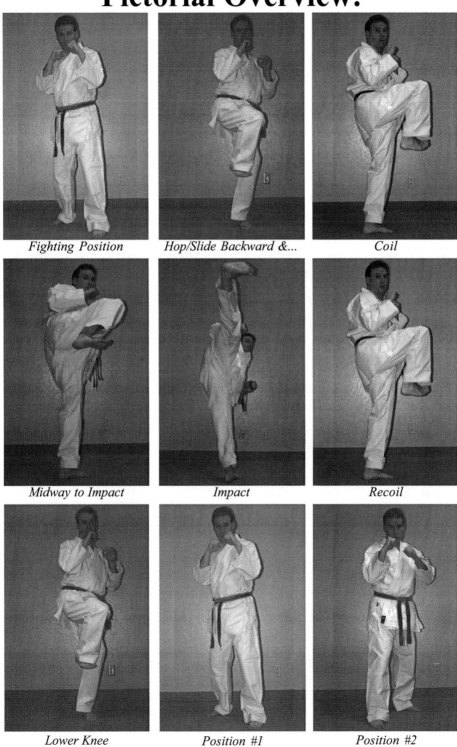

Fighting Position | Hop/Slide Backward &... | Coil

Midway to Impact | Impact | Recoil

Lower Knee | Position #1 | Position #2

Front Leg Side Kick

The Front Leg Side Kick is unique in the fact that it does not start off of the rear leg during the execution of the kick. As a matter of fact, even though this is perhaps the weakest of all the Side Kicks in this book, it is still a necessary and very effective kick. This kick is executed by shifting your weight onto your rear leg while bringing your front knee up directly in front of you and to the center into the "Raise Knee" position of this kick. With practice, this can be one of the fastest Side Kicks in your kicking arsenal.

Fighting Position:

1. Your fighting position for this kick is exactly the same as it was for Step-Behind Side Kick. With your kicking leg in the forward position to begin with rather than in the rearward position.
2. This stance is approximately shoulder width apart with the heel of your rear foot in a direct line with the heel of your front foot.
3. Your front or lead foot should be pointing directly at your opponent.
4. Your rear foot is angled toward the left at approximately a 45-degree angle. Your weight should be distributed evenly over the balls of both feet.
5. Your knees are slightly, but not noticeably bent. They should not be locked straight or rigid.
6. Your body should be facing at a 45-degree angle toward

Fighting Position
Foot Position

Fighting Position Front View

Fighting Position Side View

your opponent. This presents a smaller target area and also allows you the opportunity to initiate a faster kick.

7. Your hands should be held up (like a boxer's), with the elbows tucked in to protect the ribs and your hands up to protect your head. Your hands should remain as close to this position as possible throughout the entire kick.

8. Your head should be facing your opponent with your chin tucked down and protected by your lead shoulder.

9. Your eyes should be centered on your opponent's chest.

Raise Knee:

10. Using the toes of your kicking foot, push off the floor and bring your kicking leg knee up directly in front of you and to the center. Your knee should be at least waist high, and your kicking foot should already be in the correct position to strike your opponent.

11. As your bring your kicking leg up, your upper body should remain facing at a slight angle toward your opponent. In this position, the kicking leg side of your body should be closer to your opponent than your base leg side. Your back will remain straight but not rigid.

12. Although your hands have switched position, they should still be held up (like a boxer's), with the elbows tucked in to protect the ribs and your hands up to protect your head.

Raise Knee
Foot Position

13. Your head is up and facing towards your opponent, while your eyes remain in contact with your opponent throughout the entire kick.

Raise Knee Front View

Raise Knee Side View

Coil:

14. Your base leg foot should have moved approximately 90-degrees (counterclockwise) by pivoting on the ball of your foot.
15. Even though your body position has changed, your kicking leg knee should remain directly in front of your body, and at least waist high. While your kicking foot should be in front of and above your base leg knee.
16. Turn your body counterclockwise so that the kicking leg side of your body is now facing directly towards your opponent.

Coil Foot Position

17. Your head should still be looking over your kicking shoulder, while your eyes remain in contact with your opponent.

Coil Position Front View

Coil Position Side View

Close Up:

15a. Your kicking leg foot is slightly in front of your base leg, and as high above the knee as possible, while being tucked in close to your groin. This gives you a tighter coil and helps keep your heel on a straight and even "Path of Trajectory."

15b. The outside (knife) edge of your kicking foot is pointed down towards the ground with your big toe closest to your kicking knee, and your pinkie toe closest to the ground. This helps maintain the proper foot position, and also makes the foot and ankle more rigid when kicking.

15c. Your kicking leg calf and hamstring muscles should make considerable contact with one another in the coil position.

Close Up of Coil

116

Midway to Impact:

18. Your base leg foot should have moved approximately 20-degrees (counterclockwise) by pivoting on the ball of your foot, while your base leg knee remains slightly bent.

19. Your kicking leg knee should be pointed to the side, and in this position, be almost parallel with the ground. The heel on your kicking foot should follow a straight and even "Path of Trajectory" from the "Coil" position to "Impact."

Midway to Impact Foot Position

20. Your upper body should now start to lean over to your left at almost a 45-degree angle in relation to your body's previous upright position.

21. Your back should still be facing in the same direction as it was in the "Coil" position. That is facing at a 90-degree angle to your opponent's left. In this position, the kicking leg side of your body should be facing directly towards your opponent.

22. Although your body is now in the above position, your head should still be looking over your kicking leg shoulder, while your eyes remain in contact with your opponent.

Note: If your opponent is too far away from you, you can use footwork to adjust the distance between you and your opponent simply by moving your rearward foot closer to our lead foot prior to executing the kick.

Midway to Impact Front View   *Midway to Impact Side View*

Impact:

23. Your base leg foot should now have moved approximately 25-degrees (counterclockwise) by pivoting on the ball of your foot, while the knee on your base leg remains slightly bent. In this position, the heel of your foot will be closer to your opponent than your toes and pointing at approximately a 45-degree angle to the left of your opponent.

Impact
Foot Position

24. Notice how your kicking foot, kicking leg (with knee slightly bent), hips, back, shoulders, and head are all in a straight line at the initial moment of "Impact." Also, notice how the outside edge of your kicking foot is extended and that the toes of the kicking foot are pulled back towards your knee. This helps insure that contact with the target is made with the outside (knife) edge of the heel.

25. Your upper body should now be leaning to your left at almost a 75-degree angle in relation to your body's previous upright position, and almost parallel with the ground. At the moment of impact, your entire body should tighten to add power to the kick as your foot continues to "strike through" the target.

26. Your head should still be up and looking over the kicking leg shoulder. Eye contact with your opponent is maintained at all times.

Note: Utilize deception when fighting. Make your opponent believe that you are going to do one thing, when you really intend to do another.

Impact Front View   *Impact Side View*

Recoil:

27. Your base leg foot should now have moved approximately 45-degrees (clockwise) by pivoting on the ball of your base leg foot. Returning it to the exact same position it was in during the "Coil" position.

28. Your kicking leg foot should return along exactly the same straight and even "Path of Trajectory" it followed from the "Coil" position to "Impact." Your kicking leg foot and knee should now be in the exact same position that they were in during the "Coil" position.

29. Your upper body should straighten up from the previous position you were in during the "Impact" phase of the kick. Your back is straight, but not rigid, and is still facing at a 90-degree angle to your opponent's left. In this position, the kicking leg side of your body should be facing directly towards your opponent.

30. Your head should have remained looking over your kicking leg shoulder. Your eyes are still in contact with your opponent, whether he is still standing, or lying on the ground.

Recoil
Foot Position

Note: The principles and techniques described within this book are not specific to any particular school or style. The information supplied within this book is intended to be used by any martial artist, practicing any style, anywhere in the world.

Recoil Position Front View

Recoil Position Side View

119

Lower Knee:

31. Your base leg foot should have moved approximately 90-degrees (clockwise), by pivoting on the ball of the foot. The toes of your base leg foot should now be pointing directly at your opponent.

Lower Knee Foot Position

32. Your kicking leg and foot will now return to the "Raise Knee" position, with your kicking leg knee up in front of you and at least waist high. Your kicking foot should have remained in the correct position to strike your opponent.

33. Your upper body, which should have also began turning in a clockwise direction, is now facing at approximately a 45-degree angle to your opponent's right. Your back remains straight, but not rigid. Although your hands have switched position throughout the kick, they should still be held up (like a boxer's), with the elbows tucked in to protect the ribs and your hands up to protect your head.

34. Your head should still be up and looking over your kicking leg shoulder. Your eyes are still in contact with your opponent, whether he is still standing, or lying on the ground.

Note: Your first line of defense should be your kicks, as they are the longest and most powerful weapons in your arsenal. Kicking falls into the "Long Range" category, while punching and hand strikes fall into the "Mid Range" category. Knee and elbow strikes fall into the "Short Range" category, while joint techniques fall into your final range, "Grappling."

Lower Knee Front View

Lower Knee Side View

Return to Fighting Position:

There are two ways that you can return to a fighting position from the "Lower Knee" position. They are as follows:

Position #1

35a. After you have reached the "Lower Knee" position, simply bring your kicking foot behind you and set it down into a fighting position with your kicking leg behind you, rather than in front of you.

35b. After you have reached the "Lower Knee" position, simply leave your kicking foot in front of you and set it down into a fighting position with your kicking leg in front of you, rather than behind you.

Position #2

Note: As you can see in the illustrations presented above, the optimum angle for impact in relation to your opponents body is a 90-degree angle. Therefore, the further away you are from a 90-degree angle, the less effective your kick is going to be. For example, as you look at the illustrations on the previous page, imagine that your opponent is bent over at the waist, and you have a side view of your opponents body. The black arrows are Side Kicks delivered to your opponents solar plexus. Which one is going to be more effective, the one on the left? Or the one on the right?

121

Pictorial Overview:

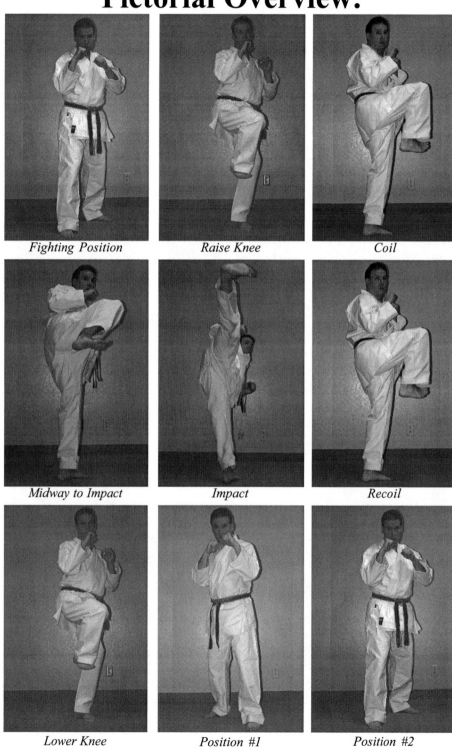

Fighting Position   *Raise Knee*   *Coil*

Midway to Impact   *Impact*   *Recoil*

Lower Knee   *Position #1*   *Position #2*

Switch Side Kick

The Switch Side Kick is identical in execution to the Back Leg Side Kick, with one notable exception. A switching motion of the feet, which is performed immediately prior to the execution of the kick. The switch is used to confuse your opponent and can also increase the power in this kick due to the added momentum of switching your feet. The starting position is the same as for Spinning Side Kick, with your kicking leg in the forward position, rather than in the rear position. The actual switching of the feet prior to execution of the kick is performed by simultaneously switching the position of both feet utilizing a straight line or scissors type motion. This results in a fighting position with your kicking leg now in the rearward position. When executing the switch, be sure and move your feet first without initially moving your upper body in order to avoid telegraphing the switch to your opponent. Your hips and upper body will begin to move immediately after your feet, but not before.

Fighting Position:

1. Your fighting position for this kick is the exact same as for Spinning Side Kick. That is your kicking leg will be in the forward position to begin with rather than in the rear.
2. This stance is approximately shoulder width apart with the heel of your rear foot in a direct line with the heel of your front foot.
3. Your front or lead foot should be pointing directly at your opponent.
4. Your rear foot is angled towards the left at approximately a 45-degree angle. Your weight should be distributed evenly over the balls of both feet.

Fighting Position Foot Position

Fighting Position Front View

Fighting Position Side View

123

5. Your knees are slightly, but not noticeably bent. They should not be locked or rigid.
6. Your body should be facing at a 45-degree angle toward your opponent. This presents a smaller target area and also facilitates a faster switch, which allows you the opportunity to initiate a faster kick.
7. Your hands should be held up (like a boxer's), with the elbows tucked in to protect the ribs and your hands up to protect your head. Your hands should remain as close to this position as possible throughout the entire kick.
8. Your head should be facing your opponent with your chin tucked down and protected by your lead shoulder.
9. Your eyes should be centered on your opponents chest.

Switch Feet & Raise Knee:

10. Utilizing a scissors type motion of your legs and feet, simultaneously switch your front foot with your rear foot and vice versa. As soon as the ball of your front foot touches the ground in the rearward position, begin to execute the kick.
11. Using the toes of your kicking foot, push off the floor and bring your kicking leg knee up in front of you and to the center. Your knee should be at least waist high, and your kicking foot should already be in the correct position to strike your opponent.
12. The kicking leg side of your body should remain closer to your opponent than your base leg side throughout the entire "switch" and execution of the kick.

Switch Feet &
Raise Knee
Foot Position

Switch Feet &... Front View

Switch Feet &... Side View

124

Coil:

13. Your base leg foot should have moved approximately 90-degrees (counterclockwise) by pivoting on the ball of your foot.

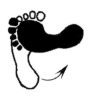

14. Even though your body position has changed, your kicking leg knee should remain directly in front of your body, and at least waist high. While your kicking foot should be in front of and above your base leg knee.

15. Turn your body counterclockwise so that the kicking leg side of your body is now facing directly towards your opponent.

Coil Foot Position

16. Your head should still be looking over your kicking shoulder, while your eyes remain in contact with your opponent.

Coil Position Front View

Coil Position Side View

Close Up:

14a. Your kicking leg foot is slightly in front of your base leg, and as high above the knee as possible, while being tucked in close to your groin. This gives you a tighter coil and helps keep your heel on a straight and even "Path of Trajectory."

14b. The outside (knife) edge of your kicking foot is pointed down towards the ground with your big toe closest to your kicking knee, and your pinkie toe closest to the ground. This helps maintain the proper foot position, and also makes the foot and ankle more rigid when kicking.

14c. Your kicking leg calf and hamstring muscles should make considerable contact with one another in the coil position.

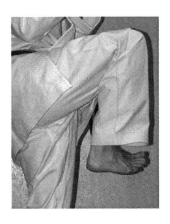

Close Up of Coil

Midway to Impact:

17. Your base leg foot should have moved approximately 20-degrees (counterclockwise) by pivoting on the ball of your foot, while your base leg knee remains slightly bent.

18. Your kicking leg knee should be pointed to the side, and in this position, be almost parallel with the ground. The heel on your kicking foot should follow a straight and even "Path of Trajectory" from the "Coil" position to "Impact."

19. Your upper body should now start to lean over to your left at almost a 45-degree angle in relation to your body's previous upright position.

20. Your back should still be facing in the same direction as it was in the "Coil" position. That is facing at a 90-degree angle to your opponent's left. In this position, the kicking leg side of your body should be facing directly towards your opponent.

21. Although your body is now in the above position, your head should still be looking over your kicking leg shoulder, while your eyes remain in contact with your opponent.

Midway to Impact Foot Position

Note: Although you have been confronted by an opponent, the decision to execute a technique, whether it is a kick, punch, throw, or joint technique should be determined by you and your alone, not by the actions or inactions of your opponent.

Midway to Impact Front View

Midway to Impact Side View

Impact:

22. Your base leg foot should now have moved approximately 25-degrees (counterclockwise) by pivoting on the ball of your foot, while the knee on your base leg remains slightly bent. In this position, the heel of your foot will be closer to your opponent than your toes and pointing at approximately a 45-degree angle to the left of your opponent.

Impact
Foot Position

23. Notice how your kicking foot, kicking leg (with knee slightly bent), hips, back, shoulders, and head are all in a straight line at the initial moment of "Impact." Also, notice how the outside edge of your kicking foot is extended and that the toes of the kicking foot are pulled back towards your knee. This helps insure that contact with the target is made with the outside (knife) edge of the heel.

24. Your upper body should now be leaning to your left at almost a 75-degree angle in relation to your body's previous upright position, and almost parallel with the ground. At the moment of impact, your entire body should tighten to add power to the kick as your foot continues to "strike through" the target.

25. Your head should still be up and looking over the kicking leg shoulder. Eye contact with your opponent is maintained at all times.

Note: You must be able to control the body's innate response to pull back or slow down when it is about to impact with something.

Impact Front View

Impact Side View

127

Recoil:

26. Your base leg foot should now have moved approximately 45-degrees (clockwise) by pivoting on the ball of your base leg foot. Returning it to the exact same position it was in during the "Coil" position.

27. Your kicking leg foot should return along exactly the same straight and even "Path of Trajectory" it followed from the "Coil" position to "Impact." Your kicking leg foot and knee should now be in the exact same position that they were in during the "Coil" position.

28. Your upper body should straighten up from the previous position you were in during the "Impact" phase of the kick. Your back is straight, but not rigid, and is still facing at a 90-degree angle to your opponent's left. In this position, the kicking leg side of your body should be facing directly towards your opponent.

29. Your head should have remained looking over your kicking leg shoulder. Your eyes are still in contact with your opponent, whether he is still standing, or lying on the ground.

Recoil
Foot Position

Note: The only time that your entire base leg foot is in contact with the ground, is in the initial "Fighting Position," during the "Impact" phase of the kick, and in the "Return to Fighting Position."

Recoil Position Front View

Recoil Position Side View

128

Lower Knee:

30. Your base leg foot should have moved approximately 90-degrees (clockwise), by pivoting on the ball of the foot. The toes of your base leg foot should now be pointing directly at your opponent.

31. Your kicking leg and foot will now return to the "Raise Knee" position, with your kicking leg knee up in front of you and at least waist high. Your kicking foot should have remained in the correct position to strike your opponent.

*Lower Knee
Foot Position*

32. Your upper body, which should have also began turning in a clockwise direction, is now facing at approximately a 45-degree angle to your opponent's right. Your back remains straight, but not rigid. Although your hands have switched position throughout the kick, they should still be held up (like a boxer's), with the elbows tucked in to protect the ribs and your hands up to protect your head.

33. Your head should still be up and looking over your kicking leg shoulder. Your eyes are still in contact with your opponent, whether he is still standing, or lying on the ground.

Note: Eventually, after you have correctly executed thousands of Switch Side Kicks, there should be little to no change at all in the position of your upper body before, during, or even after you "switch" your feet prior to kicking.

Lower Knee Front View

Lower Knee Side View

Return to Fighting Position:
There are two ways that you can return to a fighting position from the "Lower Knee" position. They are as follows:

Position #1

34a. After you have reached the "Lower Knee" position, simply bring your kicking foot behind you and set it down into a fighting position with your kicking leg behind you, rather than in front of you.

34b. After you have reached the "Lower Knee" position, simply leave your kicking foot in front of you and set it down into a fighting position with your kicking leg in front of you, rather than behind you.

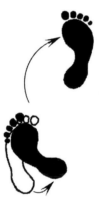

Position #2

Note: When executing a "switch" kick of any kind, compare it to the shooting action of a rifle. For example; the switching motion is the trigger of the rifle, while the ground is the firing pin. The ball of your kicking foot is the primer in the bullet casing, while the combination of muscular speed, strength, and proper technique is the gunpowder. And finally, the heel of your kicking foot is the bullet. As you squeeze the trigger (switch your feet), it releases the firing pin, which strikes the primer in the casing (the ball of your kicking foot touching the ground), and ignites the gunpowder, which fires the bullet (execute your kick) along its "Path of Trajectory," where it <u>STRIKES THROUGH</u> its target.

Pictorial Overview:

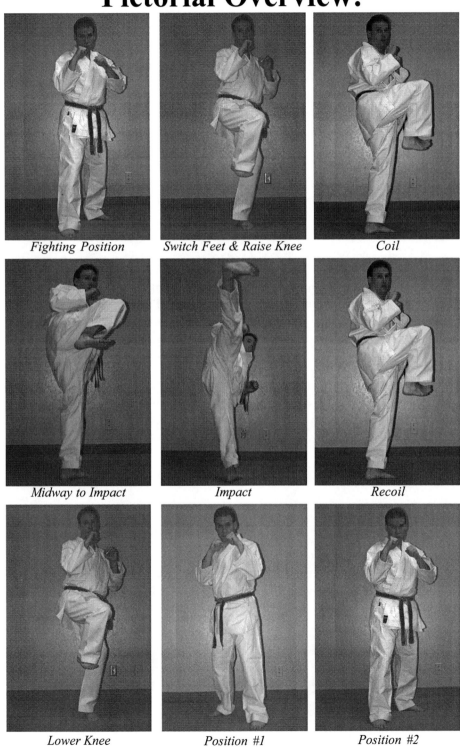

Fighting Position	*Switch Feet & Raise Knee*	*Coil*
Midway to Impact	*Impact*	*Recoil*
Lower Knee	*Position #1*	*Position #2*

Off-Setting Side Kick

The Off-Setting Side Kick is identical in execution to the Back Leg Side Kick, with one notable exception. A quick double step motion to the side (which puts you at a 45-degree angle from your original starting position), this is performed immediately prior to executing the kick. The starting position is the same as Back Leg Side Kick, in that your kicking foot is in the rear position. The actual double-step motion of the feet prior to the execution of the kick is performed by first moving the rearward foot and then the forward foot off at a 45-degree angle to the side of your opponent. When executing the double-step motion, be sure and move your rearward foot first, then your forward foot, without moving your hips and upper body in order to avoid telegraphing the move to your opponent. Your hips and upper body will begin to move when you begin to place the forward foot back onto the ground.

Fighting Position:

1. Your fighting position for this kick is the exact same as Back Leg Side Kick, in that your kicking leg will be in the rearward position.
2. This stance is approximately shoulder width apart with the heel of your rear foot directly in line with the heel of your front foot
3. Your front or lead foot should be pointed directly at your opponent.
4. Your rear foot is angled toward the right at approximately a 45-degree angle. Your weight should be distributed evenly over the balls of both feet.
5. Your knees are slightly, but not noticeably bent. They should not be locked straight or rigid.

Fighting Position Foot Position

Fighting Position Front View

Fighting Position Side View

132

6. Your body should be facing at a 45-degree angle towards your opponent. This presents a smaller target area and also facilitates a faster off-set, which allows you the opportunity to initiate a faster kick.

7. Your hands should be held up (like a boxer's), with the elbows tucked in to protect the ribs and your hands up to protect your head. Your hands should remain as close to this position as possible throughout the entire kick.

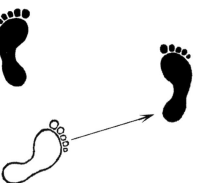

8. Your head should be facing your opponent with your chin tucked down and protected by your lead shoulder.

9. Your eyes should be centered on your opponent's chest.

Off-Set (part one):

10. Move your rear foot to the right (approximately 2-3 feet), and slightly forward (approximately 8 to 10 inches).

Off-Set Foot Position (part one)

First Step on Off-Set Front View

First Step on Off-Set Side View

Off-Set (part two) & Raise Knee:

11. Move your front foot to the right approximately 12 to 18 inches. As soon as you set your front foot down, push off the floor with your rear foot and bring your kicking leg knee directly up in front of you and to the center of your body. Your knee

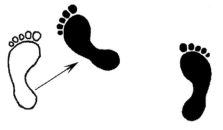

Off-Set Foot Position (part two)

should be at least waist high. Your kicking foot should already be in the correct position to strike your opponent. However, when first learning this kick, make the offsetting and the raising of the knee two separate moves.

12. Your body should now be at a 45 -degree angle from its original starting position, and you should already have raised your knee up into the "Raise Knee" position.

Raise Knee Foot Position

Second Step on Off Set Front View

Second Step on Off Set Side View

Raise Knee Front View

Raise Knee Side View

Coil:

13. Your base leg foot should have moved approximately 90-degrees (counterclockwise) by pivoting on the ball of your foot.

14. Even though your body position has changed, your kicking leg knee should remain directly in front of your body, and at least waist high. While your kicking foot should be in front of and above your base leg knee.

Coil Foot Position

15. Turn your body counterclockwise so that the kicking leg side of your body is now facing directly towards your opponent.

16. Your head should still be looking over your kicking shoulder, while your eyes remain in contact with your opponent.

Coil Position Front View

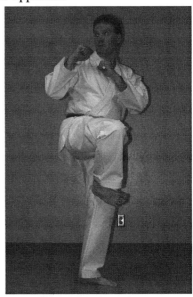

Coil Position Side View

Close Up:

14a. Your kicking leg foot is slightly in front of your base leg, and as high above the knee as possible, while being tucked in close to your groin. This gives you a tighter coil and helps keep your heel on a straight and even "Path of Trajectory."

14b. The outside (knife) edge of your kicking foot is pointed down towards the ground with your big toe closest to your kicking knee, and your pinkie toe closest to the ground. This helps maintain the proper foot position, and also makes the foot and ankle more rigid when kicking.

14c. Your kicking leg calf and hamstring muscles should make considerable contact with one another in the coil position.

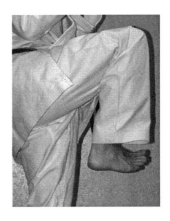

Close Up of Coil

Midway to Impact:

17. Your base leg foot should have moved approximately 20-degrees (counterclockwise) by pivoting on the ball of your foot, while your base leg knee remains slightly bent.

18. Your kicking leg knee should be pointed to the side, and in this position, be almost parallel with the ground. The heel on your kicking foot should follow a straight and even "Path of Trajectory" from the "Coil" position to "Impact."

19. Your upper body should now start to lean over to your left at almost a 45-degree angle in relation to your body's previous upright position.

20. Your back should still be facing in the same direction as it was in the "Coil" position. That is facing at a 90-degree angle to your opponent's left. In this position, the kicking leg side of your body should be facing directly towards your opponent.

21. Although your body is now in the above position, your head should still be looking over your kicking leg shoulder, while your eyes remain in contact with your opponent.

Midway to Impact
Foot Position

Note: One of the most important factors needed for the correct execution of a Side Kick, or any kick for that matter, is the proper pivoting on the ball of the base leg foot throughout the entire execution of the kick.

Midway to Impact Front View

Midway to Impact Side View

Impact:

22. Your base leg foot should now have moved approximately 25-degrees (counterclockwise) by pivoting on the ball of your foot, while the knee on your base leg remains slightly bent. In this position, the heel of your foot will be closer to your opponent than your toes and pointing at approximately a 45-degree angle to the left of your opponent.

Full Extension Foot Position

23. Notice how your kicking foot, kicking leg (with knee slightly bent), hips, back, shoulders, and head are all in a straight line at the initial moment of "Impact." Also, notice how the outside edge of your kicking foot is extended and that the toes of the kicking foot are pulled back towards your knee. This helps insure that contact with the target is made with the outside (knife) edge of the heel.

24. Your upper body should now be leaning to your left at almost a 75-degree angle in relation to your body's previous upright position, and almost parallel with the ground. At the moment of impact, your entire body should tighten to add power to the kick as your foot continues to "strike through" the target.

25. Your head should still be up and looking over the kicking leg shoulder. Eye contact with your opponent is maintained at all times.

Note: Don't over-extend your technique by "reaching" for your opponent. Create the proper distance using footwork before executing your kick.

Impact Front View

Impact Side View

137

Recoil:

26. Your base leg foot should now have moved approximately 45-degrees (clockwise) by pivoting on the ball of your base leg foot. Returning it to the exact same position it was in during the "Coil" position.

27. Your kicking leg foot should return along exactly the same straight and even "Path of Trajectory" it followed from the "Coil" position to "Impact." Your kicking leg foot and knee should now be in the exact same position that they were in during the "Coil" position.

*Recoiling
Foot Position*

28. Your upper body should straighten up from the previous position you were in during the "Impact" phase of the kick. Your back is straight, but not rigid, and is still facing at a 90-degree angle to your opponent's left. In this position, the kicking leg side of your body should be facing directly towards your opponent.

29. Your head should have remained looking over your kicking leg shoulder. Your eyes are still in contact with your opponent, whether he is still standing, or lying on the ground.

Note: The "off-setting" movement is one of the primary techniques utilized in the "8 Directions of Attack" strategy. This is a very important strategic technique and one that can be utilized in any martial art.

Recoil Position Front View

Recoil Position Side View

Lower Knee:

30. Your base leg foot should have moved approximately 90-degrees (clockwise), by pivoting on the ball of the foot. The toes of your base leg foot should now be pointing directly at your opponent.

*Lower Knee
Foot Position*

31. Your kicking leg and foot will now return to the "Raise Knee" position, with your kicking leg knee up in front of you and at least waist high. Your kicking foot should have remained in the correct position to strike your opponent.

32. Your upper body, which should have also began turning in a clockwise direction, is now facing at approximately a 45-degree angle to your opponent's right. Your back remains straight, but not rigid. Although your hands have switched position throughout the kick, they should still be held up (like a boxer's), with the elbows tucked in to protect the ribs and your hands up to protect your head.

33. Your head should still be up and looking over your kicking leg shoulder. Your eyes are still in contact with your opponent, whether he is still standing, or lying on the ground.

Note: Eventually, after you have become proficient executing the "off-set" movement and the kick independently of one another, you will want to combine the two into one continuous fluid motion.

Lower Knee Front View

Lower Knee Side View

Return to Fighting Position:

There are two ways that you can return to a fighting position from the "Lower Knee" position. They are as follows:

34a. After you have reached the "Lower Knee" position, simply bring your kicking foot behind you and set it down into a fighting position with your kicking leg behind you, rather than in front of you.

Position #1

34b. After you have reached the "Lower Knee" position, simply leave your kicking foot in front of you and set it down into a fighting position with your kicking leg in front of you, rather than behind you.

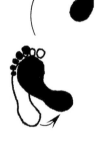

Position #2

Note: Both of these "Return to Fighting Positions," will be at a 45-degree angle to the right of your initial "Fighting Position."

Note: The Side Kick is unique in the fact that, like the Front Kick and the Roundhouse Kick, it can literally be used to strike your opponent anywhere on his body. From the ankle to the top of the head, and everywhere in-between. This makes it one of the three most versatile kicks that you can have in your personal arsenal of kicking techniques.

Pictorial Overview:

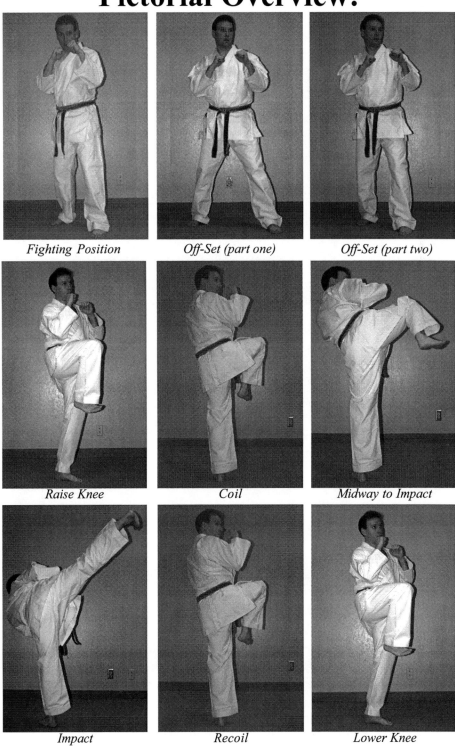

Fighting Position   *Off-Set (part one)*   *Off-Set (part two)*

Raise Knee   *Coil*   *Midway to Impact*

Impact   *Recoil*   *Lower Knee*

141

Position #1   *Position #2*

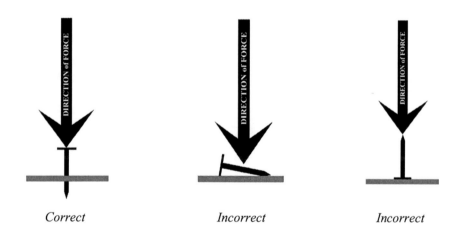

Correct   *Incorrect*   *Incorrect*

Note: As I explained to you on page 28, and have illustrated for you above, if you apply the correct striking implement to the correct vital/vulnerable point, it is like hammering a nail into a board. If however, you strike the target incorrectly without applying all of the proper principles and correct techniques, your effectiveness will be greatly reduced and you may cause more damage to yourself rather than your opponent.

Step-Back Side Kick

The Step-Back Side Kick is identical in execution to the Back Leg Side Kick, with one notable exception. A stepping backward motion, which is performed immediately prior to executing the kick. This stepping backward motion is used to draw your opponent into you, or to avoid an attack. It can also increase the power in this kick due to the added momentum of stepping backward. The actual stepping back motion of the forward foot prior to the execution of the kick, is performed by simply stepping back with the forward foot into another fighting position. Only now, the kicking leg is in the rearward position rather than in the forward position. When executing the stepping back motion, be sure and move your forward foot without initially moving your hips and upper body in order to avoid telegraphing the movement to your opponent. Your hips and upper body will begin to move as you set your foot back down on the ground.

Fighting Position:
1. Your fighting position for this kick is exactly the same as it was for Step-Behind Side Kick. With your kicking leg in the forward position to begin with rather than in the rearward position.
2. This stance is approximately shoulder width apart with the heel of your rear foot in a direct line with the heel of your front foot.
3. Your front or lead foot should be pointing directly at your opponent.
4. Your rear foot is angled toward the left at approximately a 45-degree angle. Your weight should be distributed evenly over the balls of both feet.
5. Your knees are slightly, but not noticeably bent. They should not be locked straight or rigid.

Fighting Position Front View

Fighting Position Side View

143

6. Your body should be facing at a 45-degree angle toward your opponent. This presents a smaller target area and also facilitates a faster step-back and raise knee, which allows you the opportunity to initiate a faster kick.

7. Your hands should be held up (like a boxers), with the elbows tucked in to protect the ribs and your hands up to protect your head. Your hands should remain as close to this position as possible throughout the entire kick.

8. Your head should be facing your opponent with your chin tucked down and protected by your lead shoulder.

9. Your eyes should be centered on your opponent's chest.

Step-Back & Raise Knee:

10. Step back with your front foot approximately one shoulder width into another fighting position. As soon as the ball of your front foot touches the ground in the rearward position, begin to execute the kick.

11. Using the toes of your kicking foot, push off the floor and bring your kicking leg knee up directly in front of you and to the center. Your knee should be at least waist high, and your kicking foot should already be in the correct position to strike your opponent.

12. Although your hands have switched position, they should still be held up (like a boxer's).

13. Your head is up and facing towards your opponent, while your eyes remain in contact with your opponent throughout the entire kick.

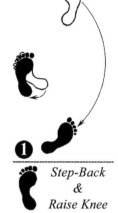

Step-Back
&
Raise Knee

Step Back & Raise Knee Front View

Step Back & Raise Knee Side View

144

Coil:

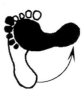

14. Your base leg foot should have moved approximately 90-degrees (counterclockwise) by pivoting on the ball of your foot.
15. Even though your body position has changed, your kicking leg knee should remain directly in front of your body, and at least waist high. While your kicking foot should be in front of and above your base leg knee.
16. Turn your body counterclockwise so that the kicking leg side of your body is now facing directly towards your opponent.
17. Your head should still be looking over your kicking shoulder, while your eyes remain in contact with your opponent.

Coil
Foot Position

Coil Position Front View

Coil Position Side View

Close Up:

15a. Your kicking leg foot is slightly in front of your base leg, and as high above the knee as possible, while being tucked in close to your groin. This gives you a tighter coil and helps keep your heel on a straight and even "Path of Trajectory."

15b. The outside (knife) edge of your kicking foot is pointed down towards the ground with your big toe closest to your kicking knee, and your pinkie toe closest to the ground. This helps maintain the proper foot position, and also makes the foot and ankle more rigid when kicking.

15c. Your kicking leg calf and hamstring muscles should make considerable contact with one another in the coil position.

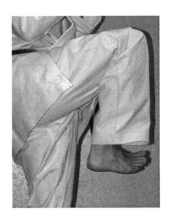

Close Up of Coil

Midway to Impact:

18. Your base leg foot should have moved approximately 20-degrees (counterclockwise) by pivoting on the ball of your foot, while your base leg knee remains slightly bent.

Midway to Impact Foot Position

19. Your kicking leg knee should be pointed to the side, and in this position, be almost parallel with the ground. The heel on your kicking foot should follow a straight and even "Path of Trajectory" from the "Coil" position to "Impact."

20. Your upper body should now start to lean over to your left at almost a 45-degree angle in relation to your body's previous upright position.

21. Your back should still be facing in the same direction as it was in the "Coil" position. That is facing at a 90-degree angle to your opponent's left. In this position, the kicking leg side of your body should be facing directly towards your opponent.

22. Although your body is now in the above position, your head should still be looking over your kicking leg shoulder, while your eyes remain in contact with your opponent.

Note: A sharp exhalation of air or KIAA!, should be executed at the initial moment of impact in order to assist in tightening your body, which in turn will help add power to your kick.

Midway to Impact Front View

Midway to Impact Side View

Impact:

23. Your base leg foot should now have moved approximately 25-degrees (counterclockwise) by pivoting on the ball of your foot, while the knee on your base leg remains slightly bent. In this position, the heel of your foot will be closer to your opponent than your toes and pointing at approximately a 45-degree angle to the left of your opponent.

Impact
Foot Position

24. Notice how your kicking foot, kicking leg (with knee slightly bent), hips, back, shoulders, and head are all in a straight line at the initial moment of "Impact." Also, notice how the outside edge of your kicking foot is extended and that the toes of the kicking foot are pulled back towards your knee. This helps insure that contact with the target is made with the outside (knife) edge of the heel.

25. Your upper body should now be leaning to your left at almost a 75-degree angle in relation to your body's previous upright position, and almost parallel with the ground. At the moment of impact, your entire body should tighten to add power to the kick as your foot continues to "strike through" the target.

26. Your head should still be up and looking over the kicking leg shoulder. Eye contact with your opponent is maintained at all times.

Note: The Side Kick should be practiced at all three kicking levels, high section, mid section and low section.

Impact Front View   *Impact Side View*

Recoil:

27. Your base leg foot should now have moved approximately 45-degrees (clockwise) by pivoting on the ball of your base leg foot. Returning it to the exact same position it was in during the "Coil" position.

28. Your kicking leg foot should return along exactly the same straight and even "Path of Trajectory" it followed from the "Coil" position to "Impact." Your kicking leg foot and knee should now be in the exact same position that they were in during the "Coil" position.

29. Your upper body should straighten up from the previous position you were in during the "Impact" phase of the kick. Your back is straight, but not rigid, and is still facing at a 90-degree angle to your opponent's left. In this position, the kicking leg side of your body should be facing directly towards your opponent.

30. Your head should have remained looking over your kicking leg shoulder. Your eyes are still in contact with your opponent, whether he is still standing, or lying on the ground.

Recoil
Foot Position

Note: The key to success in any endeavor you wish to pursue is this, self-discipline. Ask yourself this question, "Are you willing to do whatever you have to, in order to get what you want?"

Recoil Position Front View

Recoil Position Side View

Lower Knee:

31. Your base leg foot should have moved approximately 90-degrees (clockwise), by pivoting on the ball of the foot. The toes of your base leg foot should now be pointing directly at your opponent.

Lower Knee Foot Position

32. Your kicking leg and foot will now return to the "Raise Knee" position, with your kicking leg knee up in front of you and at least waist high. Your kicking foot should have remained in the correct position to strike your opponent.

33. Your upper body, which should have also began turning in a clockwise direction, is now facing at approximately a 45-degree angle to your opponent's right. Your back remains straight, but not rigid. Although your hands have switched position throughout the kick, they should still be held up (like a boxer's), with the elbows tucked in to protect the ribs and your hands up to protect your head.

34. Your head should still be up and looking over your kicking leg shoulder. Your eyes are still in contact with your opponent, whether he is still standing, or lying on the ground.

Note: One of the many exercises that I do in order to improve my kicking ability, is to try and execute as many kicks as I can correctly before setting my kicking foot back down on the ground. This exercise not only improves your kicking ability, but it is also a great way to improve your balance and your foot/eye coordination.

Lower Knee Front View

Lower Knee Side View

Return to Fighting Position:

There are two ways that you can return to a fighting position from the "Lower Knee" position. They are as follows:

35a. After you have reached the "Lower Knee" position, simply bring your kicking foot behind you and set it down into a fighting position with your kicking leg behind you, rather than in front of you.

Position #1

35b. After you have reached the "Lower Knee" position, simply leave your kicking foot in front of you and set it down into a fighting position with your kicking leg in front of you, rather than behind you.

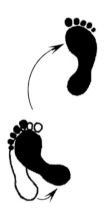

Position #2

Note: As you can see in the illustrations presented above, the optimum angle for impact in relation to your opponent's head is a 90-degree angle. Therefore, the further away you are from a 90-degree angle, the less effective your kick is going to be. For example, as you look at the illustrations above, imagine that you have not only an overhead view, but also a front view of your opponent's head. The black arrows are Side Kicks delivered to your opponent's temple. Which one is going to be more effective, the one on the left? Or, the one on the right?

150

Pictorial Overview:

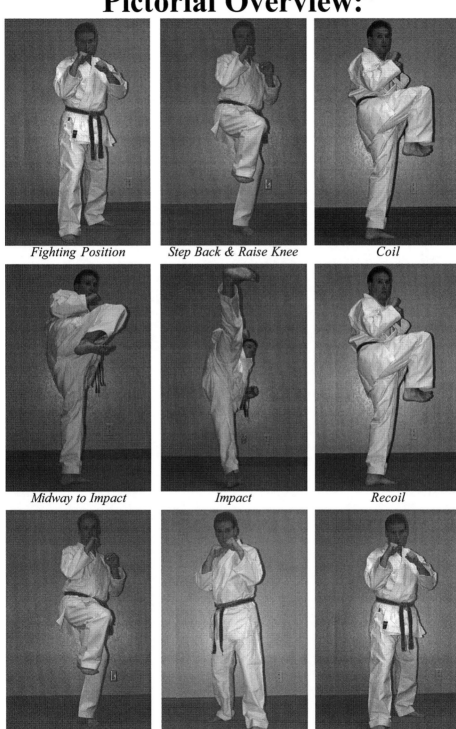

Fighting Position   *Step Back & Raise Knee*   *Coil*

Midway to Impact   *Impact*   *Recoil*

Lower Knee   *Position #1*   *Position #2*

Jumping Side Kick

The Jumping Side Kick is identical in execution to the Back Leg Side Kick, with one notable exception. That being a jumping motion that is performed immediately prior to executing the kick. This motion can be used to gain height in your kick, and it can also be used to gain distance either towards or away from your opponent. It can also increase the power in the kick due to the added momentum of jumping and kicking. The actual jumping motion is executed by bending your knees slightly and leaping either straight up, forward, or even backward depending on the situation and your opponent, in order to execute the kick. The jump itself should be practiced independently of the kick until you can execute the jump without telegraphing the kick by utilizing any unnecessary movements, such as hunching of the back and shoulders, bending of the knees too deeply, or winding up of the upper body. Remember, that this is a jumping kick, not a jump turning or a jump spinning kick. There is a difference.

Fighting Position:
1. Your fighting position for this kick is exactly the same as it is for Back Leg Side Kick. With your kicking leg in the rearward position to begin with rather than in the forward position.
2. This stance is approximately shoulder width apart with the heel of your rear foot in a direct line with the heel of your front foot.
3. Your front or lead foot should be pointed directly at your opponent.
4. Your rear foot is angled towards the right at approximately

Fighting Position Foot Position

Fighting Position Front View   *Fighting Position Side View*

a 45-degree angle. Your weight should be distributed evenly over the balls of both feet.

5. Your knees are slightly, but not noticeably bent. They should not be locked straight or rigid.

6. Your body should be facing at a 45-degree angle toward your opponent. This presents a smaller target area and also facilitates a faster jump, which allows you the opportunity to initiate a faster kick.

7. Your hands should be held up (like a boxer's), with the elbows tucked in to protect the ribs and your hands up to protect your head. Your hands should remain as close to this position as possible throughout the entire kick.

8. Your head should be facing your opponent with your chin tucked down and protected by your lead shoulder.

9. Your eyes should be centered on your opponent's chest

Raise Knee &...:

10. Using the toes of your kicking foot, push off the floor and bring your kicking leg knee up directly in front of you and to the center. Your knee should be at least waist high, and your kicking foot should already be in the correct position to strike your opponent.

11. As your bring your kicking leg up, your upper body should now be facing at a slight angle toward your opponent. In this position, the kicking leg side of your body should be closer to your opponent than your base leg side. Your back will remain straight but not rigid.

12. Your head is up and facing towards your opponent, while

*Raise Knee
Foot Position*

Raise Knee Front View

Raise Knee Side View

your eyes remain in contact with your opponent throughout the entire kick.

...Jump & Coil:

13. Moving both feet simultaneously, jump straight up and turn your body counter-clockwise 180-degrees. While you are in the air, the following things should be done simultaneously. They are as follows:

13a. Turn your head and look over your kicking shoulder. Eye contact with your opponent is maintained at all times.

13b. Bring your kicking leg knee up, to the "Coil" position.

13c. Keep your hands up throughout the entire kick.

13d. Your back should be straight, but not rigid.

13e. The kicking leg side of your body should be facing directly towards your opponent. Execute the kick.

Note: Remember, that a Jumping Side Kick can also be performed either moving forward or backward while jumping up into the air. It can also be executed off of the front leg (similar to a Front Leg Side Kick), as well as the back leg. You can also turn it into a Flying Side Kick by taking a few steps prior to jumping up into the air. Look for separate volumes in the Achieving Kicking Excellence series that deal exclusively with aerial kicks.

Jump & Coil Front View *Jump & Coil Side View*

Midway to Impact:

14. Your base leg should start to come up so that your non-kciking foot is tucked in close to protect the groin area. Your kicking leg knee should be pointed to the side, and in this position, be almost parallel with the ground. The heel on your kicking foot should follow a straight and even "Path of Trajectory" from the "Coil" position to "Impact."

15. Your upper body should remain in the upright position. You should not lean over your base leg as if you were doing a ground based kick.

16. Your back should still be facing in the same direction as it was in the "Coil" position. That is facing at a 90-degree angle to your opponent's left. In this position, the kicking leg side of your body should be facing directly towards your opponent.

17. Although your body is now in the above position, your head should still be looking over your kicking leg shoulder, while your eyes remain in contact with your opponent.

Note: Throughout the entire kicking sequence, you can see that my arms are held up and close to my body, they are not flapping around like a bird. However, if you look at the photograph below and on the right and also the same photograph in the "Impact" section, you will see that my left arm is out a bit further from my body than it should be. If you find yourself doing this, remember that it is incorrect and a quite common mistake that many martial artists make when kicking. Always keep your arms up and close to you body.

Midway to Impact Front View   *Midway to Impact Side View*

155

Impact:

18. Your base leg foot should now be tucked up towards the groin. Similar to how your kicking leg was in the "Coil" position.

19. Notice how your kicking foot, kicking leg (with knee slightly bent), hips, back, shoulders, and head are all in a straight line at the initial moment of "Impact." Also, notice how the outside edge of your kicking foot is extended and that the toes of the kicking foot are pulled back towards your knee. This helps insure that contact with the target is made with the outside (knife) edge of the heel.

20. Your upper body should still remain in the upright position. Your back remains straight, but not rigid. At the moment of impact, your entire body should tighten to add power to the kick as your foot continues to "strike through" the target.

21. Your head should still be up and looking over the kicking leg shoulder. Eye contact with your opponent is maintained at all times.

Note: The optimum moment for initial impact with the target is at approximately 75% of full extension, and at the peak of the jump.

Impact Front View   *Impact Side View*

Recoil:

22. Your base leg foot should now have straighened out and returned to the ground. With the inside edge of your foot facing towards your opponent.

23. Your kicking leg foot should return along exactly the same straight and even "Path of Trajectory" it followed from the "Coil" position to "Impact." Your kicking leg foot and knee should now be in the exact same position that they were in during the "Coil" position. Only now your base leg foot is on the ground.

24. Your upper body, which should have remained upright during the "Impact" phase of the kick, is still facing at a 90-degree angle to your opponent's left. In this position, the kicking leg side of your body should be facing directly towards your opponent.

25. Your head should have remained looking over your kicking leg shoulder. Your eyes are still in contact with your opponent, whether he is still standing, or lying on the ground.

Recoil
Foot Position

Note: If you performed the "Recoil" correctly, your kicking foot should start to retract before your non-kicking foot touches the ground.

Recoil Position Front View

Recoil Position Side View

Lower Knee:

26. Your base leg foot should have moved approximately 90-degrees (clockwise), by pivoting on the ball of the foot. The toes of your base leg foot should now be pointing directly at your opponent.

27. Your kicking leg and foot will now return to the "Raise Knee" position, with your kicking leg knee up in front of you and at least waist high. Your kicking foot should have remained in the correct position to strike your opponent.

Lower Knee
Foot Position

28. Your upper body, which should have also began turning in a clockwise direction, is now facing at approximately a 45-degree angle to your opponent's right. Your back remains straight, but not rigid. Although your hands have switched position throughout the kick, they should still be held up (like a boxer's), with the elbows tucked in to protect the ribs and your hands up to protect your head.

29. Your head should still be up and looking over your kicking leg shoulder. Your eyes are still in contact with your opponent, whether he is still standing, or lying on the ground.

Note: There are no superior techniques, only superior technicians. There are no superior martial arts, only superior marital artists.

Lower Knee Front View

Lower Knee Side View

Return to Fighting Position:

There are two ways that you can return to a fighting position from the "Lower Knee" position. They are as follows:

30a. After you have reached the "Lower Knee" position, simply bring your kicking foot behind you and set it down into a fighting position with your kicking leg behind you, rather than in front of you.

Position #1

30b. After you have reached the "Lower Knee" position, simply leave your kicking foot in front of you and set it down into a fighting position with your kicking leg in front of you, rather than behind you.

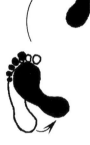 

Position #2

Note: Due to the very nature and difficulty in effectively executing a Jumping Side Kick on a standing, mentally focused opponent. I strongly recommend utilizing this kick as a finishing technique on a disoriented and preferably already injured opponent. As a general rule-of-thumb, just as a boxer sets up his opponent with several jabs before unloading a straight cross or hook. You too should also set up your opponent with easier and faster techniques before attempting a Jumping Side Kick on him.

Pictorial Overview:

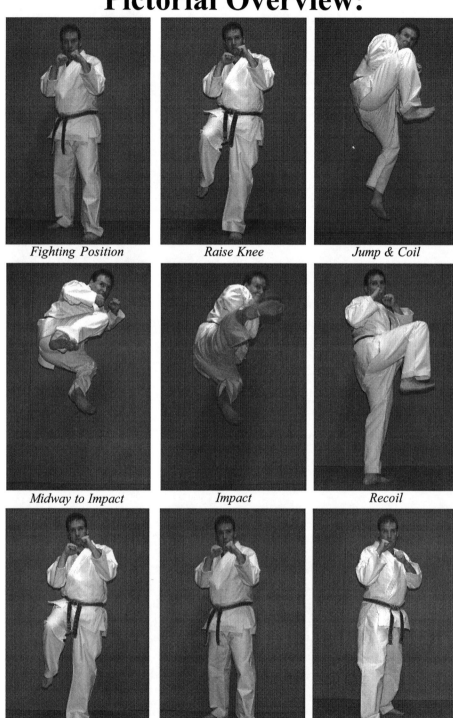

Fighting Position   Raise Knee   Jump & Coil

Midway to Impact   Impact   Recoil

Lower Knee   Position #1   Position #2

160

Step-Behind Side Kick
(With the left leg)

Here is an example on how to change the instructions presented in this book in order to execute the exact same kicks with the left leg. First of all you're going to be kicking with the left leg, rather than the right. So your rear foot and body position will be exactly opposite of those that you would use if you were kicking with the right leg. To put it simply, kicking with the left leg should mirror exactly those kicks performed with the right leg and vice versa.

Fighting Position:
1. Your fighting position for this kick is the exact same as for Back Leg Side Kick. Although your kicking leg will be in the forward position to begin with rather than in the rear.
2. This stance is approximately shoulder width apart with the heel of your rear foot in a direct line with the heel of your front foot.
3. Your front or lead foot should be pointing directly at your opponent.
4. Your rear foot is angled towards the right at approximately a 45-degree angle. Your weight should be distributed evenly over the balls of both feet.
5. Your knees are slightly, but not noticeably bent. They should not be locked or rigid.

Fighting Position
Foot Position

Fighting Position Front View

Fighting Position Side View

161

6. Your body should be facing at a 45-degree angle toward your opponent. This presents a smaller target area and also facilitates a faster step-behind, which allows you the opportunity to initiate a faster kick.
7. Your hands should be held up (like a boxer's), with the elbows tucked in to protect the ribs and your hands up to protect your head. Your hands should remain as close to this position as possible throughout the entire kick.
8. Your head should be facing your opponent with your chin tucked down and protected by your lead shoulder.
9. Your eyes should be centered on your opponents chest.

Step-Behind:

10. Keeping your upper body and hips as still as possible, step forward and behind the back of your lead leg foot with your rear leg foot.
11. When you place your rear foot back down on the ground, it should be approximately 8 to 12 inches in front of your lead foot, with the toes of your rear foot aligned with the center of your lead foot.
12. As soon as the ball of your rear foot touches the ground, begin to execute the kick.
13. Your eyes should still be centered on your opponent's chest.

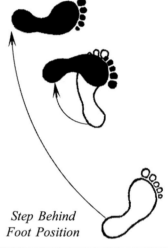

Step Behind
Foot Position

Step Behind Front View

Step Behind Side View

162

Coil:

14. Your base leg foot should have moved approximately 90-degrees (clockwise) by pivoting on the ball of your foot.

15. Even though your body position has changed, your kicking leg knee should remain directly in front of your body, and at least waist high. While your kicking foot should be in front of and above your base leg knee.

Coil
Foot Position

16. Turn your body clockwise so that the kicking leg side of your body is now facing directly towards your opponent.

17. Your head should still be looking over your kicking shoulder, while your eyes remain in contact with your opponent.

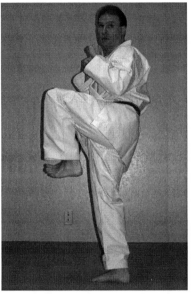

Coil Position Front View

Coil Position Side View

Close Up:

15a. Your kicking leg foot is slightly in front of your base leg, and as high above the knee as possible, while being tucked in close to your groin. This gives you a tighter coil and helps keep your heel on a straight and even "Path of Trajectory."

15b. The outside (knife) edge of your kicking foot is pointed down towards the ground with your big toe closest to your kicking knee, and your pinkie toe closest to the ground. This helps maintain the proper foot position, and also makes the foot and ankle more rigid when kicking.

15c. Your kicking leg calf and hamstring muscles should make considerable contact with one another in the coil position.

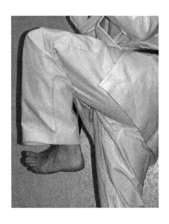

Close Up of Coil

163

Midway to Impact:

18. Your base leg foot should have moved approximately 20-degrees (clockwise) by pivoting on the ball of your foot, while your base leg knee remains slightly bent.

19. Your kicking leg knee should be pointed to the side, and in this position, be almost parallel with the ground. The heel on your kicking foot should follow a straight and even "Path of Trajectory" from the "Coil" position to "Impact."

*Midway to Impact
Foot Position*

20. Your upper body should now start to lean over to your left at almost a 45-degree angle in relation to your body's previous upright position.

21. Your back should still be facing in the same direction as it was in the "Coil" position. That is facing at a 90-degree angle to your opponent's left. In this position, the kicking leg side of your body should be facing directly towards your opponent.

22. Although your body is now in the above position, your head should still be looking over your kicking leg shoulder, while your eyes remain in contact with your opponent.

Note: If you are like the vast majority of martial artists, you will have one leg that is very good at kicking and the other that seems to lag behind. One thing that I do to correct this, is to perform 15 repetitions on my weak leg for every 10 repetitions that I perform with my strong leg. This works well for me and is a training technique you may want to try yourself.

Midway to Impact Front View

Midway to Impact Side View

Impact:

23. Your base leg foot should now have moved approximately 25-degrees (clockwise) by pivoting on the ball of your foot, while the knee on your base leg remains slightly bent. In this position, the heel of your foot will be closer to your opponent than your toes and pointing at approximately a 45-degree angle to the left of your opponent.

*Impact
Foot Position*

24. Notice how your kicking foot, kicking leg (with knee slightly bent), hips, back, shoulders, and head are all in a straight line at the initial moment of "Impact." Also, notice how the outside edge of your kicking foot is extended and that the toes of the kicking foot are pulled back towards your knee. This helps insure that contact with the target is made with the outside (knife) edge of the heel.

25. Your upper body should now be leaning to your left at almost a 75-degree angle in relation to your body's previous upright position, and almost parallel with the ground. At the moment of impact, your entire body should tighten to add power to the kick as your foot continues to "strike through" the target.

26. Your head should still be up and looking over the kicking leg shoulder. Eye contact with your opponent is maintained at all times.

Note: When kicking to the head, imagine that your opponent's head is a cue ball, and that your leg is a pool cue. Strike correctly, and sink that shot!

Impact Front View　　　　　*Impact Side View*

Recoil:

27. Your base leg foot should now have moved approximately 45-degrees (counterclockwise) by pivoting on the ball of your base leg foot. Returning it to the exact same position it was in during the "Coil" position.

28. Your kicking leg foot should return along exactly the same straight and even "Path of Trajectory" it followed from the "Coil" position to "Impact." Your kicking leg foot and knee should now be in the exact same position that they were in during the "Coil" position.

29. Your upper body should straighten up from the previous position you were in during the "Impact" phase of the kick. Your back is straight, but not rigid, and is still facing at a 90-degree angle to your opponent's left. In this position, the kicking leg side of your body should be facing directly towards your opponent.

30. Your head should have remained looking over your kicking leg shoulder. Your eyes are still in contact with your opponent, whether he is still standing, or lying on the ground.

Recoil
Foot Position

Note: At the end of your workout, execute a Side Kick as slow as you can, while maintaining strict form and control. Pay close attention to how each body part feels while executing each individual phase of the kick.

Recoil Position Front View　　　　　　*Recoil Position Side View*

Step Back Across:

31. Your kicking leg foot should return along the exact same path it followed from the "Step-Behind" position to the "Coil" position. Start by setting your kicking foot down in front of, and across your lead foot.

32. When you place your kicking foot back down on the ground, it should be approximately 8 to 12 inches behind your base leg foot, with the toes of your base leg foot aligned with the center of your kicking foot. As soon as the ball of your kicking foot touches the ground, begin to return to a fighting position.

Step Back Across Foot Position

33. Your upper body and back should still be in relatively the same position that they were in during the "Recoil" phase of this kick.

34. Your head should still be looking over your kicking leg shoulder, with your eyes in contact with your opponent, whether he is still standing, or lying on the ground.

Note: When kicking to the body, imagine that your leg is a battering ram and that your opponent's body is a large castle door. Smash that castle door until it breaks down and exposes more vital/vulnerable points to attack.

Step Back Across Front View

Step Back Across Side View

Return to Fighting Position:

35. Pivoting 90-degrees (counterclockwise) on the ball of your kicking leg foot, step back with your base leg foot into your original fighting position.

36. Your upper body will return to facing at a 45-degree angle toward your opponent.

37. Your hands should still be held up (like a boxer's), with the elbows tucked in to protect the ribs and your hands up to protect your head. Your hands should have remained as close to this position as possible throughout the entire kick.

38. Your head should still be facing your opponent with your chin tucked down and protected by your lead shoulder.

38. Your eyes, as always, remain in contact with your opponent.

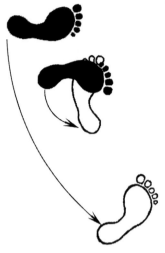

Return to Fighting Position Foot Position

Note: Although I haven't demonstrated it here, you don't have to return to your original "Fighting Position" after you "Recoil" your kicking leg. If the situations warrants it, you can set your foot down and forward into another fighting position, instead of stepping back across your base leg. However, extreme caution must be exercised as now you are stepping in towards your opponent, which is inherently more dangerous.

Return to Fighting Position Front View   *Return to Fighting Position Side View*

Pictorial Overview:

Fighting Position

Step-Behind

Raise Knee & Coil

Midway to Impact

Impact

Recoil

Step Back Across

Return to Fighting Position

169

Training and Practice Methods

The following practice methods in this section, when performed correctly and consistently, are designed to improve your skill, speed, and power when executing the Side Kick. However, whether or not you improve is dependent solely upon you and your commitment to your training. When performing the exercises and drills that follow, concentrate on form and technique rather than speed or power.

Skill

The precise movement and skill you wish to obtain in the ring and on the street should be practiced correctly and consistently during training.

In other words, how you practice and train in the dojo is how you will react in the ring or on the street.

Kicking skills must be practiced correctly and consistently, or speed and technique will begin to deteriorate.

Your kicking skills can be likened to an automobile. With proper maintenance and care, your automobile will last a lifetime. However, if you neglect your automobile, it will break down on you when you need it most. You never can tell when you will suddenly need those skills. Now let's take a look at some of my favorite training exercise that I use in order to improve my Side Kick.

Mirror:

The mirror is without a doubt my favorite training aid. It enables me to see myself clearly and analyze my technique in minute detail. I can then correct any flaws as they become evident.

Training Partner:

Training with a partner is an invaluable way to practice since a partner can tell you if you are making a mistake when executing your kick. Partners can also hold bags and pads for kicking, as well as, making the entire work out more enjoyable. A word of caution though, if your training partner spends a good deal of time talking and less time working out, then perhaps it is time to search for a new partner. Idle chatter should have no place in your training regimen. A focused workout session on your own is infinitely preferable to one spent with a poor partner.

Three Dimes:

Begin by taking three dimes and placing them on the floor. One under the pivot point on the ball of your base leg foot, and the second under the center of your base leg heel. The third dime is placed in the exact position where your base leg heel will make contact with the ground during the moment of impact. Execute a Back Leg Side Kick. At the moment of impact, your base leg heel should have come to rest exactly on the third dime (Figure #1). As you continue with your kick, your base leg

170

heel should return to its original starting position by once again coming to rest exactly on the second dime (Figure #2). This exercise, when practiced correctly and consistently, will greatly improve the pivoting skills needed to properly execute a Side Kick.

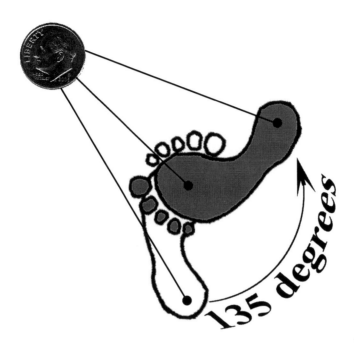

Figure #1

Figure #2

Wall Practice:

This exercise, to improve my Side Kick, was first demonstrated to me over twenty years ago. It is still valid today and should be an important part of your training program. This exercise is very simple to perform and focuses primarily on the "Coil," "Path of Trajectory," "Impact," and the "Recoil" of the kicking leg.

Start by placing your non-kicking hand on the wall at approximately shoulder height. Look over your kicking leg shoulder. Slowly bring your kicking leg knee up to the "Coil" position. Once your kicking leg is in the "Coil" position, extend your kicking leg from the "Coil" position up to the "Impact" position. Immediately after you have made initial impact with your target, be sure and "Strike Through" your target and then bring your kicking leg back into the "Coil" position.

After you have completed the above mentioned actions, you will finish this practice method by returning your kicking foot back down to its original starting position. This is a very important part of the kick and should never be skipped. As with all Wall and Chair Practice Methods, concentrate on form and technique rather than speed or power.

You can increase the level of difficulty when performing the Wall Practice Method by attaching ankle weights to your legs before performing the exercises. However, a word of caution, you must practice your kicks more slowly and pay very close attention to form. **Do Not** perform the Side Kick at full speed with ankle weights on. If you do, you are asking for trouble and a possible knee or hip injury. Practice hard, but practice smart.

Another variation is to practice total relaxation of the body throughout the entire kicking sequence, except at the moment of impact. Upon impact tighten every muscle in your body from your toes to your fingertips. As soon as you have impacted with your target, relax your body again. Start slow, and gradually increase speed. This will help prepare your body to deliver the maximum amount of force to the target. This takes a lot of practice, so be patient and the results will come.

Note: One hundred repetitions performed correctly is ten times better than one thousand repetitions performed incorrectly! Always remember, the quantity is nowhere near as important as the quality. This applies to every facet of life, not just the martial arts.

Starting Position

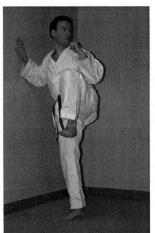

Coil

Midway to Impact

Impact

Begin Recoil

Recoil

Return to Starting Position

173

Chair Practice:

This is a terrific practice method to perform in order to perfect your kicking skills when utilizing the Side Kick. Perform a Back Leg Side Kick like you normally would, and then utilize the chair to maintain your balance while working to perfect your technique. As with the Wall Practice Method, you should concentrate on improving your form and technique rather than speed or power. You can increase the level of difficulty when performing the Wall or Chair Practice Method by attaching ankle weights to your legs before performing the exercises. However, a word of caution, you must practice your kicks more slowly and pay very close attention to form. **Do Not** perform the Side Kick at full speed with ankle weights on. If you do, you are asking for trouble and a possible knee or hip injury. Practice hard, but practice smart. Another variation is to practice total relaxation of the body throughout the entire kicking sequence, except at the moment of impact. Upon impact tighten every muscle in your body from your toes to your fingertips. As soon as you have impacted with your target, relax your body again. Start slow, and gradually increase speed. This will help prepare your body to deliver the maximum amount of force to the target. This takes a lot of practice, so be patient and the results will come.

Remember, that you must practice each kick that you learn 5,000 to 10,000 times correctly, before you can be proficient at it. And then you must practice on a regular basis to maintain that skill level. Practice does not make you perfect, but it sure does help.

Fighting Position

Twist & Grab Chair

174

Coil

Midway to Impact

Impact

Begin Recoil

Recoil

Return to Fighting Position

Strength

Nearly every movement in the martial arts is carried out in opposition to a resistance. Therefore, an increase in strength means an improvement in performance.

"Stronger muscles give the athlete greater movement potential. If everything is equal, the stronger athlete will be bigger, faster, more flexible, more enduring, and less prone to injury." —Dr. Ellington Darden

"One of the benefits of strength is that it acts as a shock absorber for a muscle. Most injuries, such as tennis elbow, are caused by a force or succession of forces that cause the muscle to exceed its tensile strength. When that happens, the muscle tears. The stronger you are, the less likely that is to happen." —Michael Quinn

In order to increase muscular strength and endurance, the muscles must be worked harder than normal.

Your legs carry you everywhere you go, and are approximately 10 times stronger than your arms. Therefore the stronger your legs are, the stronger you are.

Although I have included only a few specific leg exercises in this volume, I consider the following exercises to be some of the best available for adding strength to not only your Side Kicks, but all of your other kicks as well. In subsequent volumes in the Achieving Kicking Excellence series, I will include several additional leg exercises which, depending on how you perform them, can develop either strength or endurance depending on the amount of weight used and repetitions performed. As with all exercises, train hard, but train smart.

Squats-with weights:

Squats are perhaps the single best overall strength building exercise there is for the entire body, and most assuredly the best exercise there is for the lower body. The muscles emphasized during the squat are the quadriceps, gluteus maximus, lower back and the hamstrings. Ideally, you should use a squat rack and training partner every time you perform this exercise. However, not all of us have access to a health club or weight training facility. Therefore, the utmost in caution must be exercised when lifting weights by yourself. You should never lift heavy weights without someone present to spot for you. Always wear shoes, weight lifting gloves and a weight lifting belt for support when you are weight lifting.

Before you begin, make sure that the weighted plates are securely fastened to the end of the bar. It is also a good idea to have a padded wrap around the center portion of the bar, where it rests across the back of your shoulders during the execution of this exercise. Bending your knees and keeping your back straight, squat down and grasp the bar with a comfortable grip. Your legs should be approximately shoulder width apart with your toes pointed slightly outward. Straighten your legs to a standing position while lifting the bar up to your chest. Press the bar over your head and then carefully lower it behind your neck until it is resting on the back of your shoulders as seen in the starting position.

From this position, slowly bend your legs, allowing your knees to move outward in the same direction as your toes. At the same time contract your back muscles in order keep your body rigid as your perform this exercise. Slowly squat down until

176

you are in a full squat position with your thighs parallel to the ground. Once you have reached the full squat position, slowly stand up to the starting position. Repeat this movement as often and as safely as you can.

Remember:

1. Keep your back straight throughout the entire movement.
2. Focus your eyes on a spot at head level in order to help keep your head up.
3. Do not bounce at the bottom of the squat.
4. Do not squat lower than your thighs parallel to the floor.
5. Do not use heavy weights without a squat rack and spotters present.

Training Routine:

1. For strength use a heavier weight and perform three sets of 8 to 12 repetitions.
2. For endurance use a lighter weight and perform three to five sets of 15 to 20 repetitions per set.
3. Perform this exercise no more than 3 times per week.

Starting & Finishing Position

Squat Position

Hack Squat Machine:

Squats are perhaps the single best overall strength building exercise there is for the entire body, and most assuredly the best exercise there is for the lower body. The muscles emphasized during the squat are the quadriceps, gluteus maximus, lower back and the hamstrings. The Hack Squat is a variation of the basic squat, and is an excellent means of isolating the leg muscles. This exercise is used by many weightlifters when they have no spotter available, or when they can no longer safely perform free weight squats because their back or legs are too tired or sore. Remember, you should always wear shoes, weight lifting gloves and a weight lifting belt for support when you are weight lifting.

Before you begin, make sure that the weighted plates are securely fastened to the machine. Step into the machine and place your back against the padded surface, while wedging your shoulders beneath the padded yokes attached to the front of the machine. Your legs should be straight and your feet should be approximately 6 to 10 inches apart and parallel with each other. Firmly grasp the handles located on the sides of the machine. Keeping your back straight, reach down and release the safety bar.

From this position, slowly bend your legs, allowing your knees to move outward in the same direction as your toes. At the same time contract your back muscles in order keep your body rigid as your perform this exercise. Slowly squat down until you are in a full squat position with your thighs parallel to the ground. Once you have reached the full squat position, slowly stand up to the starting position. Repeat this movement as often and as safely as you can. This exercise primarily emphasizes the quadriceps. However, if you place your feet closer together, you will place more emphasis on the gluteal muscles. If you spread your feet further apart, you will place more emphasis on the adductors.

Remember:
1. Keep your back straight throughout the entire movement.
2. Focus your eyes on a spot at head level in order to help keep your head up.
3. Do not bounce at the bottom of the squat.
4. Do not squat lower than your thighs parallel to the foot, or base plate.
5. Inhale as you are performing the squat, and exhale as you are straightening your legs.

Training Routine:
1. For strength use a heavier weight and perform three sets of 8 to 12 repetitions.
2. For endurance use a lighter weight and perform three to five sets of 15 to 20 repetitions per set.
3. Perform this exercise no more than 3 times per week.

178

Starting & Finishing Position

Squat Position

179

Inclined Leg Press:

The Inclined Leg Press is another variation of the standard squat, which places little to no pressure on the back. Therefore, if you have back problems which preclude you from executing a standard squat, you can use this exercise as a substitute. The muscles emphasized during the leg press are the same as they are for the squat, they are the quadriceps, gluteus maximus, and the hamstrings. This exercise is used by many weightlifters when they have no spotter available, or when they can no longer safely perform free weight squats because their back or legs are too tired or sore. Remember, you should always wear shoes, weight lifting gloves and a weight lifting belt for support when you are weight lifting.

Before you begin, make sure that the weighted plates are securely fastened to the machine. Step into the machine and sit down placing your back against the padded surface, while placing your butt on the padded seat. Your legs should be straight and your feet should be approximately shoulder width apart and parallel with each other. Firmly grasp the handles located on the sides of the machine. Keeping your legs straight, reach down and release the safety bar.

From this position, slowly bend your legs, allowing your knees to move slowly towards your chest. As your knees move toward your chest, make sure that they move to the outside of your chest and not directly at the chest itself. Once your knees have reached the appropriate distance from your chest, press your legs upward and return to the starting position. Repeat this movement as often and as safely as you can. Placing your feet low on the plate or closer together, primarily emphasizes the quadriceps. However, if you place your feet farther apart, you will place more emphasis on the adductors. If you place your feet high on the plate, you will place more emphasis on the gluteals and hamstrings.

Remember:
1. **Using too heavy of a weight can cause damage to the hip and pelvic area.**
2. As with all exercises, exhale during the execution of the movement, and inhale as you return to your original starting position.
3. Do not raise your butt up, always keep your butt on the padded seat!
4. Do not lower the weight too close to your chest before pressing upward.
5. Do not bounce at the top or bottom of the movement.

Training Routine:
1. For strength use a heavier weight and perform three sets of 8 to 12 repetitions.
2. For endurance use a lighter weight and perform three to five sets of 15 to 20 repetitions per set.
3. Perform this exercise no more than 3 times per week.

Starting & Finishing Position

Squat Position

181

Seated Calf Machine:

This exercise places primary emphasis on the soleus muscle, which is located below the gastrocnemius, and is attached under the knee joint and connects with the calcaneus by the Achilles tendon. This exercise can be performed on a specially designed seated calf machine, or on a regular bench by placing your toes and the balls of your feet on a block of wood, and then placing a padded barbell across your lower thighs just above the knees. Before starting this exercise, make sure that the proper amount of weight is securely attached to the machine, or to the barbell.

Begin by sitting on the machine's seat and place the padded bar firmly across the lower portion of your thighs. Place your toes and the balls of your feet on the foot bar. Keeping your back straight, let your hands rest upon the top of the padded bar. Slowly raise your heels up and carefully release the safety bar located on the side of the machine. Slowly lower your heels as far below the level of your toes as possible. Hold this position for a moment. Then slowly raise them up as high as you can. Repeat this movement as often and as safely as you can.

Remember:
1. Perform this exercise slowly in order to obtain the maximum benefit.
2. Do not do partial movements. Utilize the entire range of motion on this exercise.

Training Routine:
1. For strength use a heavier weight and perform three sets of 8 to 12 repetitions.
2. For endurance use a lighter weight and perform three to five sets of 15 to 20 repetitions per set.
3. Perform this exercise no more than 3 times per week.

Starting & Finishing Position

Toe Raise Position

Side-to-Side Squats with weights:

Begin by standing with your feet approximately shoulder width apart, toes pointed out at a slight angle. Lift the barbell safely and place it behind your head and across your shoulders. Your hands should maintain a wide grip on the bar for better balance. Keep your back straight and your head up throughout the entire exercise. From this position, slowly spread your feet out to approximately two to three shoulder widths apart. Slowly squat down with one leg, until you are in a side squat position. Once you have reached the side squat position, your squatting leg thigh should be parallel with the floor, while your non-squatting leg is straight out to the side. Slowly return to the starting position, and repeat this movement on the opposite side. Repeat this movement as often and as safely as you can.

Remember:
1. Keep your back straight and rigid throughout the entire movement.
2. Focus your eyes on a spot at head level in order to help keep your head up.
3. **Use light weights only,** and do not bounce at the bottom of the squat.

Training Routine:
1. This is primarily an endurance building exercise and should be performed with a high number of repetitions (30 to 100) for several sets (3 to 10).
2. Perform this exercise no more than 3 times per week.

Starting & Finishing Position

Pre-Squat Position

Side Squat Position to the Right

Side Squat Position to the Left

Cable Machine Side Kicks:

Cable Machine Side Kicks are designed to work on all of the leg muscles utilized in executing the Side Kick. This exercise also increases strength in the abdomen and lower back. Before you begin, make sure that the ankle strap is securely fastened to your ankle, and that the cable is securely attached to the ankle strap. It is also a good idea to have a thick sock on so that the ankle strap doesn't rub against your leg during the execution of this exercise. The performance of this exercise is identical to the Wall Practice method described on page 172. Use light weights to start with and perform 3 to 5 sets of 25 to 30 repetitions per set. Perform this exercise no more than 3 times per week.

Starting & Finishing Position

Coil & Recoil Position

Impact Position

Side-to-Side Squats:

This exercise, along with the variation using weights described on page 183, are perhaps two of the best overall leg exercises that you can do in order to improve the strength in your legs for kicking, especially for the Side Kick. Begin by standing with your feet approximately two to three shoulder widths apart, toes pointed out at a slight angle. Your hands can be either behind your head, or resting on your hips. Keep your back straight and your head up throughout the entire exercise. From this position, slowly squat down with one leg, allowing your knee to move outward in the same direction as your toes. At the same time contract your back muscles in order keep your body rigid as your perform this exercise. Slowly squat down until you are in a full side squat position with your squatting leg thigh parallel to the ground, and your non-squatting leg straight out to the side. Once you have reached the side squat position, slowly return to the starting position, and repeat this movement on the opposite side. Repeat this movement as often and as you safely can.

Remember:
1. Keep your back straight throughout the entire movement.
2. Focus your eyes on a spot at head level in order to help keep your head up.
3. Do not bounce at the bottom of the squat.
4. Do not squat lower than your thigh parallel with the floor.

Training Routine:
1. This is primarily an endurance building exercise and should be performed with a high number of repetitions (30 to 100) for several sets (3 to 10).
2. Perform this exercise no more than 3 times per week.

Starting & Finishing Position

Side Squat Position to the Right Side

Side Squat Position to the Left Side

Plyometric High Knee Raises:

Plyometric high knee raises are without a doubt one of the best exercises to perform in order to add explosive power to your kicks. This exercise emphasizes all of the muscles of the leg to a certain degree, from the muscles of the foot all the way up to the gluteus maximus and lower back. When performing this or any other plyometric type exercise, you should exercise extreme caution due to the amount of stress that is placed on your body from these exercises. I would advise you to perform these exercises no more than two times per week, and to give yourself at least two days rest in between each plyometric training routine. Before you begin, make sure that the area around you is clear of any obstacles.

This exercise can be performed with or without shoes. Make sure that you are wearing gi bottoms or other loose fitting pants. Begin by standing with your feet approximately shoulders width apart and your toes pointing forward. Keeping your back straight and your head up, bring your arms up into a fighting position with your hands at shoulder level. From this position, explosively bring one of your knees up as high as you can to your upper chest. As soon as your knee reaches your chest, explosively force your leg back down to the ground, but don't slam your foot into the ground. Set it down gently, but quickly. As soon as your foot touches the ground, immediately and explosively repeat the same movement with your opposite leg. Repeat this movement as often and as safely as you can alternating your legs each time.

Remember:

1. Make sure that the area around you is free of any obstacles.
2. Focus your eyes on a spot at head level in order to help keep your head up.
3. Do not slam your foot into the ground. Set it down quickly, but gently.
4. Your back should be kept as straight as possible at all times.
5. Do not perform plyometric type exercises more than twice per week.

Training Routine:

1. Perform one set of 10 to 20 repetitions per leg, no more than 2 times per week.
2. Work up to two sets of 20 to 50 repetitions per leg, no more than 2 times per week.

Starting Position

High Knee Position

Return to Starting Position

High Knee Position

Incorrect High Knee Position

188

Speed

The speed of your kicks during training should be at the same speed you plan to use during self-defense or competition.

As I stated earlier in this section, how you practice and train in the dojo is how you will react in the ring or on the street.

The primary component of speed under pressure is not physical, but mental. Therefore, you must stay focused and concentrate.

Your mind controls your body. Therefore, you must keep control of your mind in order to perform at your optimum level.

If you think that you're slow, you will be slow. However, if you believe that you can be faster, you will be faster.

Now let's take a look at some of my favorite speed training exercises that I use to increase the speed in my Side Kicks.

Ankle Weights:

This is my favorite piece of exercise equipment that I use in order to improve the speed of not only my Side Kicks, but all other kicks as well. Properly used, ankle weights can improve your speed and hitting power in your legs, as well as, increasing muscular stamina. Improperly used however, they can cause a variety of injuries to the joints and connective tissues. This is not only detrimental to your body, but it also causes you to lose valuable training time. When practicing your kicks with ankle weights, you should make sure that they are securely fastened around your ankles and not loose. Start with 2 lbs. on each ankle and gradually build up the weight over time. Don't rush it. Perform your kicks no faster than 3/4 speed. Concentrate on technique and form, rather than speed and power. Remember that your legs will weaken faster utilizing the ankle weights. Therefore, caution must be exercised so that you do not injure your knees or hips. Any kicking drill or exercise can be utilized with ankle weights, with the notable exceptions of plyometric exercises and reactionary drills. I do not recommend using any kind of weight what-so-ever when performing plyometric exercises. These exercises are of such high intensity that no additional weight is needed. Reactionary drills require you to kick as fast as you can in response to an outside stimulus. Therefore, ankle weights would be a hindrance rather than a benefit.

Quick Draw:

This is an excellent reactionary drill and requires the use of a training partner. I got the idea of this training method from watching western movies when I was a kid. Picture the following scene from any western movie.

The sheriff looks out the window of the saloon onto the dust-covered Main Street of town where the outlaw who killed his father stands waiting. A tied down six-gun slung low on his right thigh. The sheriff steps through the saloon doors and out onto the porch, his eyes never leaving the outlaw. He walks off the porch and out onto the street where he turns toward the outlaw. They stand facing each other from no more than 50 feet. Neither one moves. Suddenly the outlaw makes a move for his gun. BANG! The outlaw falls backward, dead, a .45 caliber bullet lodged in his brain.

The sheriff holsters his Colt Peacemaker and walks back into the saloon.

Now you may be asking yourself how is this going to help your kicking skills. The answer is really quite simple. I have modified the classic western shoot out, or quick draw, by utilizing a training partner and your kicks instead of a Colt Peacemaker. Begin by having your training partner stand in front of you out of kicking range. You will be facing him in a fighting position. At your partner's discretion, he will make a prearranged movement, which will be the indicator for you to execute a kick as quickly as you can toward your partner. That indicator can be anything from a snapping of the fingers to the blinking of an eye.

Use your imagination. Kicks can be performed one at a time, two or three at a time, using the same leg or alternating legs. Be creative and design your own unique routine. This exercise can also be utilized with a heavy bag or force pad. However, extreme care must be utilized so that you do not accidentally miss your target and end up hitting your training partner. That doesn't seem to go over to well with training partners.

Water Training:

This particular training method requires a rather large piece of training equipment, a full-sized swimming pool. The deep end of the pool needs to be at least 6 feet deep in order for you to practice your kicks in mid-chest to shoulder deep water. This method of practicing your kicking technique is identical to the Wall Practice Method. After you have become sufficiently proficient with the Wall Practice Method, you can then begin to practice the primary kick and all of its variations including the aerial kicks. However, always keep in mind that when you are practicing in water, you will always be kicking against a constant state of resistance.

Start off by practicing your kicking technique at 1/4 speed until your kicking skills become easier and more natural. As you become progressively more efficient in your kicking skills, you will gradually increase your speed until you are performing your kicks at full speed. Even though you are practicing in the water, never sacrifice proper technique for speed or power.

It is imperative that you take all necessary precautions when practicing this technique. If at all possible, utilize this training method only with a training partner in case of any unforeseen accidents.

Jump Rope:

Jumping rope is not only a time-honored method for building endurance in the sport of boxing, but it is also an excellent method of building rhythmic foot movement and speed for all sports that require foot and hand coordination.

Proper Repetitive Practice:

Regardless of the activity, the more you practice the faster you will become, provided proper technique is maintained throughout the exercise. Notice the difference in the speed of your kick from the very first time you practice it, to the 1,000th time, the 5,000th time, the 10,000th time, etc. Which one was faster?

Power

Force = Mass x Acceleration

In other words, the faster you are, multiplied by the greatest amount of muscular mass that you can generate behind your kick, equals striking power. Now let's take a look at my two favorite pieces of training equipment that I utilize in order to improve my kicking power. They are the force bag (hand held kicking shield) and the heavy bag.

Force Bag:

The force bag or kicking shield is a hand held pad or bag, that is usually made out of vinyl or leather with a foam filled core. There are usually two sets of handles located on the bag, two on the back portion of the bag, and one on each side of the bag. For most people, one bag is sufficient in order to prevent injury to the bag holder when kicking. However, for those of us that kick considerably harder, you may want to duct tape two bags together in order to sufficiently protect your bag holder. If utilized correctly, these bags are invaluable as training aids in order to increase the speed and power in your Side Kick.

Begin by having your bag holder grasp the handles located on the sides of the bag. He should hold the bag firmly against his chest and stomach. He should position himself in a solid forward stance with his legs about shoulder width apart and his rear leg about 1-1/2 or 2 shoulder widths from his front leg. As the kicker, you want to aim your kicks at the center of the bag. At all times you must be extremely careful when kicking so that you do not accidentally kick your training partner. They tend to get a little grouchy when kicked.

As the bag holder, you do not want to get in the habit of being just a bag holder. Utilize this time to improve your defensive skills by relaxing your body the entire time until just before the moment of impact. Make sure that the bag is facing directly at the kicker. It should not be at an angle, for this can cause injury to the kickers knee if his kick slides off of the target. You can utilize any kicking routine you can think of with the force bag. You can practice single kicks, multiple kicks (one leg at a time or alternating legs), the Quick Draw Method, etc. You are only limited by your own imagination.

Heavy Bag:

The heavy bag is a great piece of training equipment because it never gets tired, it doesn't show up late for practice and generally speaking you cannot hurt it. Best of all it loves to take a beating. You can utilize full force Side Kicks on the heavy bag without worrying about hurting it. However, you must exercise caution when kicking so that you don't inadvertently hurt yourself by hyper-extending your knee, twisting an ankle, etc., when kicking the heavy bag. There are numerous routines, which you can utilize when working on the heavy bag. Some of the routines I utilize in order to improve my Side Kicks are exactly the same as those utilized when kicking the force bag. However, when utilizing the heavy bag, you generally do not have a training partner holding the bag and therefore the bag must be allowed to swing freely after being hit, in order to simulate an actual moving opponent.

191

Running:

Running is a must for anyone who is serious about self-defense or competition. I will not go into any details about running itself other than to say that it should be an essential part of any martial artists training program. There are several good books on running available, and any one of them would be an invaluable addition to your library.

Running Stairs:

In addition to regular running, running stairs is an excellent method of building the muscles in the legs while at the same time building up your aerobic capacity and endurance. However, extreme caution must be exercised at all times to avoid injuring yourself while performing this or any exercise described in this book.

Relaxation and Tension:

Muscle contractions used during training should duplicate those used in self-defense or competition.

If you do not utilize the proper tension and relaxation principles in the gym when kicking, you will not use them correctly on the street or in the ring. This principle is very simple yet seems to be very difficult for individuals to follow. Physiologically speaking a relaxed muscle is able to react faster than a tense muscle. Therefore you want to remain as relaxed as possible from the time you initiate your kick until just before the moment of impact. At this point your entire body should tighten up to add power to your kick. Immediately after the moment of impact, your muscles should once again relax in order to recoil as quickly as possible from your target. I have found that the best method for practicing this technique is to perform the Wall Practice Method, which I described earlier in this section. Perform this technique slowly and concentrate on proper technique while remaining totally relaxed throughout the kicking process until just before the moment of impact. At this point tighten all of the muscles in your body and hold them that way for just an instant. Remember once impact has been made, relax immediately and recoil your kicking leg.

Trouble Shooting Guide

In this chapter, I will present some of the most common questions concerning mistakes that I have encountered from students when attempting to perform the Back Leg Side Kick or any one of its many variations. I will then attempt to provide a generalized answer to each of those questions. Although one must keep in mind that there is no way to provide the appropriate answer to each person without actually seeing him or her perform the kick in person. When you have a problem, always refer back to the instruction section that covers that particular movement in which you are having a problem. One of my instructors once imparted upon me a small piece of wisdom that I would now like to share with you concerning mistakes. "If you suddenly find yourself making mistakes, go back to the beginning." In other words, you can never practice or study the basic techniques enough, for they are the foundation in which all other techniques are based.

Why do I always seem to be hitting with the wrong part of my foot?

This is usually caused by one of three things. (1) You are not brining your toes back and towards your shin exposing the outside (knife) edge of your heel as the striking implement. This happens quite often when one tries to "reach" for the target, rather than having already created the proper striking distance. (2) You are not bringing the kicking knee up into the proper "Coil" position before executing the kick. This tends to make the kicking leg "swoop" when executed, rather than following the correct "Path of Trajectory" towards the target. When your kicking leg "swoops," your ankle or the outside top of your kicking foot is usually what strikes the target instead of the outside (knife) edge of the heel. (3) You are not turning completely sideways to your opponent prior to the execution of the Side Kick and the front of your body, rather than your side is facing towards your opponent. This would naturally make the striking surface of your foot the outside edge of the pinkie toe area, rather than the outside (knife) edge of the heel.

Why do I always seem to be hitting low every time I kick?

This particular problem is almost exclusively caused by one thing. You are attempting to kick from the ground in a "swooping" motion rather than bringing the knee of the kicking leg up into the proper "Coil" position. One other possibility is that you may not be leaning your body slightly backward over your base leg prior to fully extending the kicking leg.

Every time I try and use a Side Kick with a training partner, they always seem to see it coming and move out of the way!

This particular problem can be related not only to improper technique, but also to inappropriate use of the Side Kick. Let's look at technique first. (1) You may not be coiling fast enough prior to the execution of the kick, or you may be making some unconscious body movement prior to executing the kick, and therefore, are telegraphing your intentions to you opponent. (2) Another possible problem is that you may not yet have the entire sequence of movements flowing together to where they all are one continuous motion. You may be pausing during the execution of the kick and not be aware of it. The best way to correct both of these problems is to practice in front of a mirror. (3) The other possibility is that your technique is fine, but your application of the kick is incorrect. Are you attempting to use the Side Kick offensively? Or, defensively? Remember, that for the most part, the Side Kick is a defensive technique, rather than an offensive technique. Although it can effectively be used in both instances. Try limiting your use of the kick when sparring and always try and set up the Side Kick by utilizing another technique before executing it. Whether it is another kick, punch, or even simply footwork.

My Side Kick always seems to glance off the target whether it's in a tournament or in the dojo!

This can be caused by many different things. More often than not, it is the result of improper use of the Side Kick and/or improper coiling of the kicking leg. Two other points to remember. (1) You must maintain eye contact with your opponent throughout the entire execution of the kick. (2) Your opponent (if he is smart) is not going to stand there and let you hit him. He is going to be trying to hit you while trying to avoid getting hit himself. This is why thousands of correct repetitions of this or any kick is only the beginning. Sparring is perhaps the best way to find out what will, and what will not, work in any given situation. This applies to everything, not just kicking.

Why do my Side Kicks miss the target more times that they hit it?

The most common solution to this problem is that you have to make sure that you are looking at your opponent during the entire time you are executing the kick. Stay focused! Another possible solution is that you need to practice the coil, full extension to impact, and recoil, portions of the kick more often and slower until your accuracy improves.

It seems like every time I hit a solid target, I get knocked back farther that my target does!

This can most often be attributed to a person "pushing" his opponent with the kick, rather than "striking through" his opponent. In order to correct this you need to work on two primary areas. (1) Recoiling the kicking leg faster after impact, and (2) Practicing the relaxation and tension movements before, during, and after impact.

I can do a Back Leg Side Kick fairly well, but when it comes to some of the other Side Kicks, I always seem to have problems!

The important thing to remember here is that all of the Back Leg Side Kick variations are based on the primary kick, Back Leg Side Kick. If you are executing the Back Leg Side Kick correctly, then you need to focus more of your attention on not only the additional moves associated with each particular variation, but also in

194

the ability to flow in a continuous fluid motion from the additional portion of the particular Side Kick variation, to the Back Leg Side Kick itself.

Why do I lose my balance every time I kick?

There are several possible reasons for this. (1) You may not be keeping your head up and looking over your kicking leg shoulder while executing the kick. (2) You may be attempting to imitate a bird by waving your arms all over the place instead of having them in control and next to your body. (3) Your center of gravity may not be over your base leg. (4) Over-extending "reaching" with the kicking leg. (5) Leaning to far backward with your upper body during the execution of the kick. (6) Balancing on the ball of your foot, rather than the entire base foot when impacting with the target.

How come I just can't seem to get any power into my Side Kick?

Power in a Side Kick is generated by the correct execution of all phases of the kick. The most important being proper technique. For arguments sake, let us assume (and you know what happens when you make an assumption) that you are performing all of the "movement" phases of the kick correctly. I would then have to say that you are probably not performing the relaxation and tension portion of the kick correctly, as this is the most difficult aspect of the kick to perform correctly. Remember, that the entire body should be in a relaxed state throughout the entire execution of the kick, except immediately before impact. When the entire body should turn into a solid, rigid mass to support and add power to the kick, and then immediately relax again to add speed to the recovery or recoil.

Why is my Side Kick so slow?

Anything is slow the first few hundred or even a thousand times you do them. Speed is not important to learning, be patient and practice until the kick becomes instinctive in nature. After you become comfortable with the execution of the kick, then you can gradually add more speed when executing it. If you are still experiencing a slow kick, you may be too tense when executing the kick and this will greatly decrease your speed. Another potential problem could be that you "see" yourself as being slow. If you want to be fast, think fast!

Why do I always seem to land off-balance?

There are several possible reasons for this, and it may be a combination of these instead of just one. (1) You are over-extending "reaching" with your kicking leg. (2) Your center of gravity is not over your base leg. (3) You are trying to impact with the target while balancing on the ball of your base foot, rather than the entire foot itself.

Remember that often times we are unable to see clearly are own mistakes. That is why a qualified and competent instructor, and a good training partner is so vitally important to your martial arts training.

Side Kick Applications

In this chapter, I will discuss some of the basic applications for the Back Leg Side Kick and the ten variations discussed in this book. Please keep in mind that the numerous applications of each kick could fill an entire book. Therefore I will limit this section to one application per kick. A second series of books detailing the combat and tournament applications of each kick is in the works and will be published following the release of this ten volume series. Keep in mind that the photographs in this section are staged in order to give you the best possible view of each technique in order to help you learn from them. The actual execution of any of these kicks should be one continuous motion and should be executed instantaneously without thought. My assistant and I have intentionally made some errors that can be seen in some of these photographs in order to help you correct some common mistakes. See if you can spot them before I tell you them at the end of each kicking application.

For reference purposes, Ron Dunlap will be the attacker, while I will be the defender in this series of photographs. Ron is wearing a black uniform, while I am wearing a white uniform.

Turning Side Kick:

1. You and your opponent are facing each other in what is commonly referred to as a Closed Position, meaning that in this case, each of you has your left leg forward and the front of your bodies facing in different directions. In this case, the front of Ron's body is basically facing toward the camera, while the front of my body is facing away from the camera.

2. As you can see, Ron initiates his attack by attempting to punch me in the head with his left hand. Notice how his weight shifts over his left leg as he leans forward. As soon as you sense your opponent's attack, begin to initiate your kick.

3. Always execute all phases of the kick correctly in order to achieve maximum effectiveness. Remember to protect yourself at all times and not to telegraph your intentions to your attacker.

4. Execute the kick. Take a close look at my kicking leg, notice how I am at approximately 95% of full-extension. This is not where you generate the maximum amount of effectiveness when striking an opponent. This kick was not much more than a hard push or slap, not a penetrating impact like it should have been. Remember to immediately retract your kicking leg after impact.

Did you notice anything wrong or improper in this series of photographs? Take another look. See them now?

Look at photograph number one; see how I am still in a fighting position and not moving after Ron has already begun to throw his punch. This is not a good thing to do. As soon as I sensed Ron's committed attack, I should have already kicked him before he got to that position.

Now take a look at photographs number two and three; notice how Ron's punch is fully extended, while I am still in the beginning stages of executing this kick. I can not stress this enough, always strive to kick faster than you can blink!

And finally, take a close look at photograph number four; to start with, I struck Ron at approximately 95% of full extension, rather than the much more effective 75% of full extension. Doing this not only lessens the potential power in my kick, but it also makes my kick little more than a hard slap or push, rather than the devastating penetrating impact is should have had. If I had properly executed all phases of the kick correctly, my kicking foot should have ended behind Ron's head (before recoiling), not where it ended up in the photograph.

Front Leg Side Kick:

1. You and your attacker are facing each other in what is commonly referred to as an Open Position, meaning that one of you has his left leg forward while the other has his right leg forward. This would result in both of your bodies facing in the same direction. In this case, the front of both Ron and I's bodies are basically facing toward the camera.

2. Your opponent initiates his attack by stepping towards your. Notice how Ron's feet are coming closer together. Which, if you paid attention earlier in this book, tells you that Ron's base of support is going to get a lot smaller.

3. Sensing his impending attack, you begin to execute the kick. Remember to maintain eye contact with your attacker.

4. Execute the kick. As you can see in this photograph, I struck Ron on his lead leg that was bearing most of his weight as he moved forward. Resulting in him being stopped dead in his tracks, and leaving him in a very vulnerable position. Ideally, you want to strike your opponent when he is midway through his technique.

Did you notice anything wrong or improper in this series of photographs? Take another look. See them now?

Look at photograph number four; notice how I have stopped Ron's forward momentum by striking him where the leg joins the lower torso. However, you can also see how dangerous it is for me to leave my kicking leg "hanging" in the air. See how easy it would be for Ron to grab it.

No matter how you add it up, ninety-nine pennies do not add up to one dollar. All aspects of a properly executed kick are much like pennies in a dollar. Every one of the one hundred pennies must be present in order to have a complete dollar, just like every aspect of a kick must be performed correctly in order to have a proper kick. As you look at this picture, ask yourself this question, "What additional techniques could I use after my initial kick?"

Switch Side Kick:

1. Once again, you and your attacker are facing each other in what is commonly referred to as an Open Position, meaning that one of you has his left leg forward while the other has his right leg forward. This would result in both of your bodies facing in the same direction. In this case, the front of both Ron and I's bodies are basically facing toward the camera.

2. Sensing Ron's attack, I not only switch my feet, but I also add a hop/slide backwards in order to avoid his attack, and to create more distance between us.

3. Begin to initiate your kick. Notice how open Ron's body is, especially with his right arm fully extended. Watch for your opponents mistakes, and then capitalize upon them. Remember to keep your hands up and to protect yourself at all times.

4. Execute your kick. As you can clearly see in this photograph, look at the greater distance that can be covered with the leg compared to the arm.

Did you notice anything wrong or improper in this series of photographs? Take another look. See them now?

First off, remember that you can execute either a Back Leg Side Kick, or a Turning Side Kick after the initial switch.

Now take a close look at photograph number three; notice how Ron's punch is fully extended exposing the entire right hand side of his body from his shoulder down, as well as, the entire front of his body. In this particular situation, Ron's body is wide open to a wide variety of kicking and punching techniques, not just a Side Kick.

As you look at photograph number four; you can clearly see that my kicking leg is fully extended with a strike to Ron's head. Even though, in my opinion, there were a lot better targets available to strike in this particular situation. Kicking to the head when it is at its normal "high section" level can be very effective, but it can also be very dangerous. Every situation is going to be different. Therefore, you must have a complete and thorough understanding of every aspect of a technique before attempting to actually use it in a self-defense situation. That is why knowing the **WHO, WHAT, WHERE, WHEN** and **WHY's** of kicking is just as important as knowing **HOW** to kick.

Off-Setting Side Kick:

1. Once again, you and your opponent are facing each other in a Closed Position. In this case, the front of my body is basically facing toward the camera, while the front of Ron's body is facing away from the camera.

2. Your opponent begins to lunge forward in a classic wrestling attempt to grab my lead leg and wrestle me to the ground.

3. As you sense your opponent's impending attack, you begin to offset his attack by moving your right foot to the right and at a 45-degree angle to your opponent. Which you immediately follow with...

4. Moving your left leg to the right, which will effectively move your body out of the line of attack. In addition, you are also in a very advantageous position to execute various assorted counterattacks on your attacker. Remember to keep your hands up and protect yourself at all times. **Don't get lazy!** As soon as your left foot moves into position...

5. ...begin to initiate your kick. Remember to maintain eye contact with your attacker at all times.

6. Execute your kick. Ideally you want to strike your attacker while he is off balance. As seen in this picture. Notice how Ron's body is leaning too far forward, while his entire body weight is over his left leg. Not only is this position very unstable, but it also leaves Ron very vulnerable to attack. Bad for Ron, but great for me! This kick would have been even more effective if I had been a little bit closer to Ron before kicking.

Did you notice anything wrong or improper in this series of photographs? Take another look. See them now?

If you look closely at photograph number two; you will see that Ron has already initiated his attack, yet I still haven't moved in response to his attack. **This is not only incorrect, but also very dangerous!** As soon as I sensed Ron's impending attack, in photograph number one, I should have off-set immediately as I have demonstrated in photograph number four. Now look closely at photographs number three, four, and five; in photographs number three and four, I still have not begun to execute my kick, even though I have already off-set Ron who's attempting to tackle me and get me on the ground. Now when you take a look at photograph number five; you see Ron's arms are full extended in his attempt to grab my legs, and I have just now begun to execute my Side Kick.

The position of my body in photograph number five, should actually be in photograph number three, while the execution of the kick depicted in photograph number six should actually be in photograph number four.

This response from me in this series of photographs is so slow, that Ron could almost sit down at a table and enjoy a healthy lunch before my kick would come anywhere near him. You must constantly strive to have your kicks so fast, that neither you nor your opponent knows that you have thrown the kick, until after it strikes your opponent.

Step-Behind Side Kick:

1. You and your opponent are facing each other in an Open Position. However, at the moment, you are not in an effective kicking range.

2. Sensing your opponents impending attack, you step-behind your lead foot with your rear foot. This in effect "closes the distance" between you and your opponent, and puts you in an effective kicking range. However, a word of caution, do not leave your feet and legs crossed for any longer than a fraction of a second.

3. As soon as the ball of your rear foot touches back down on the ground, begin to initiate your kick. Remember to keep your hands up and protect yourself at all times. **Don't get lazy!**

4. Execute your kick.

Did you notice anything wrong or improper in this series of photographs? Take another look. See them now?

Take a look at photograph number two; see how my feet and legs are crossed. This is an extremely dangerous position to be in, and should only be executed with the utmost speed and technical perfection of movement in order to be effective. Remember, even though all of these kicks have been broken down into separate individual steps, they will eventually be executed instinctively and in one continuous fluid motion without thought and faster than the eye can blink. This skill is not easy to obtain, it takes thousands upon thousands of correctly executed kicks, along with a highly developed warrior mentality in order to achieve it. Its not impossible, it just takes a lot of hard work.

Now take a real close look at photograph number four; once again, notice how my kicking leg is fully extended, but this time I haven't even made any contact with Ron. As a matter of fact, my foot is about one inch away from Ron's face. This is what is called "posing" your kick. It may look pretty, but it frankly isn't worth a damn. No matter how technically perfect your kick is, it isn't going to do you a damn bit of good if you don't "strike through" your target. This kick may look great for a magazine cover, but it isn't worth spit in a self-defense situation.

Step-Back Side Kick:

1. You and your opponent are facing each other in an Open Position. Your opponent attempts to punch you with his right hand.

2. Sensing your opponents impending attack, you step-back in order to avoid his attack. This will also have the added benefit of increasing the distance between you and your opponent, which in turn will allow you the opportunity to execute your kick. As soon as your lead leg steps back, and the ball of your foot touches the ground,...

3. ...begin to initiate your kick. Once you've stepped back, you have the option of executing either a Back Leg Side Kick, or even a Turning Side Kick. Whichever the situation may call for. Remember that you never want to sacrifice technique for speed.

4. Execute your kick.

Did you notice anything wrong or improper in this series of photographs? Take another look. See them now?

They should be so obvious to you by now that you could see them a mile away. In case you didn't catch them, I will point them out for you. First off look at Ron's punch in photograph number three; it is fully extended and a mere 3 to 4 inches away from my lead hand. I could easily grab Ron's arm and pull him towards me in order to make my kick even more effective. Secondly, look at my kicking leg; it looks more like 95%, rather than 75% of full extension. Next, if you look really close at my kicking foot in photograph number four; you can see that I struck Ron correctly with the outside (knife) edge of my heel, rather than my toes or the center outside edge of my foot. What is going to inflict more damage to your opponent, kicking him with your heel or your toes? Which is going to hurt you less, kicking someone with your heel or your toes? If you answered your heel to both questions continue reading. If you answered your toes, go back to chapter three and reread that section.

And finally, take a close look at the target area that I struck on Ron. Is this a very effective target area? Wouldn't I have had a much more effective kick if I had struck Ron in the knee, rather than the front of his thigh. Do you see anything else? Maybe the fact that I have (once again) left my kicking leg "hanging" out in the air when I should have quickly got it back down on the ground after kicking.

Back Leg Side Kick:

1. You and your opponent are facing each other in a Closed Position. Although you are not currently in an effective punching range, you are in an effective kicking range.

2. Sensing your opponents impending attack, you take the initiative and begin to initiate your kick. Here is a little food for thought. Remember, that it is always best to avoid a confrontation, and if you can't avoid it, to end it as quickly and as decisively as possible.

3. In order to keep from telegraphing your kick to your opponent, try and keep your upper body as straight and as upright as possible until the "Midway to Impact" phase of the kick. At this point, lean slightly over your base leg to add height and power to your kick. Never sacrifice technique for speed. Remember the fable about the tortoise and the hare?

4. Execute your kick. Always remember, even though you can kick high, doesn't mean that you have to kick high. More often than not, your initial kicks in a self-defense situation will be much more effective when used at targets waist high or lower.

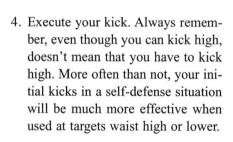

Did you notice anything wrong or improper in this series of photographs? Take another look. See them now?

If you look closely at photograph number two; you can clearly see that if I execute my kick from this position, that I will miss Ron by approximately 18 to 24 inches. Therefore, as you can see in photograph number three, I added a hop/slide forward to my kick in order to close the distance with Ron and make my kick more effective. Remember, "If it works, use it. If it doesn't work now, it may work later."

Spinning Side Kick:

1. You and your opponent are facing each other in an Open Position. However, at the moment, you and your opponent are a few steps away from one another.

2. Suddenly, your opponent starts to move towards you. Sensing your opponents attack as he moves forward, you also take a step forward in order to meet your opponents attack. As you step forward, your opponent attempts to punch you with his left hand.

3. Using the momentum gained by stepping forward, and as soon as the ball of your rear foot touches down on the ground, you want to begin turning in order to execute your Turning Side Kick. Notice how I am now looking over my kicking leg shoulder as I start my turn. Always maintain eye contact with your opponent at all times.

4. Begin to initiate your kick. Notice how I am just out of Ron's punching range.

5. Execute your kick. Now you can really see the extended range I have using my legs compared to Ron using his arms. You can also see how leaning slightly over your base leg moves your upper body away from your opponents attack.

Did you notice anything wrong or improper in this series of photographs? Take another look. See them now?

If you look closely at photographs number two, three, and four; you can see that as I stepped forward, Ron also stepped forward and threw a punch with his left hand. Meanwhile, my response was so slow that I have barely begun to initiate my kick and Ron has already completed his punch. As soon as I sensed Ron's attack, I should have already stepped forward and begun turning in preparation to execute my kick.

One of the reasons why I always say, "When you sense an attack," instead of "When you see him attack," is so that you do not rely on sight alone. Utilize all of your senses when fighting. Remember the old saying, "An ounce of prevention is worth a pound of cure." It's much easier to learn these things now, rather than later when it may be too late.

Now take a very close look at photograph number five; I realize that it is almost impossible to see, but in this photograph, I have struck Ron perfectly with the outside (knife) edge of my heel on one of the correct vulnerable points on his jaw. However, it is not going to have the effect it would have, had I struck Ron at approximately 75% of full extension, rather than at 95%. Accuracy doesn't mean diddly if you hit your target with a squirt gun, instead of a high powered rifle.

You should constantly strive to improve the accuracy of your kicks until you can hit an area the size of a dime every time you kick.

Hopping/Sliding Forward Side Kick:

1. You and your opponent are facing each other in a Closed Position. However at the moment your opponent is just out of kicking range.

2. You begin to initiate your kick. As you bring your knee up into the "Coil" position, hop or slide forward while executing your kick. Remember, you will want to initially strike your opponent at the exact moment that you end your hop or slide forward.

3. You can cover anywhere from a few inches to two feet with a correctly executed hop or slide. The exact distance will vary from application to application, but one factor remains. You must be exact in judging the correct distance or your kick will not attain its maximum effectiveness.

4. You should be executing your kick so that it initially strikes your opponent at 75% of full-extension, and at the same time you reach the end of your hop or slide forward.

Did you notice anything wrong or improper in this series of photographs? Take another look. See them now?

Look at photograph number two; notice how I am in the "Coil" position and I still have not moved forward toward my opponent. Your hop/slide forward, and coil, and kick should all be executed simultaneously, with the kick being executed at the precise moment your hop/slide forward ends. Over-extending and/or jamming the kicking leg is usually the result of misjudging the distance between you and your opponent. With this kick you have to be very precise in judging distance, or else you will end up with a very ineffective kick. Did you notice the placement of this kick?

Hopping/Sliding Backward Side Kick:

1. You and your opponent are facing each other in a Closed Position. However, at the moment your opponent is too close to you for you to kick effectively. Although you are in an effective punching and/or grappling range.

2. As your opponent attempts to punch you with his right hand, you hop or slide backward just enough to put you into an effective kicking range, and to avoid your opponents attack.

210

3. Immediately after hopping or sliding backward, bring your kicking leg up into the "Coil" position in preparation for initiating your kick. You can cover anywhere from a few inches to two feet with a correctly executed hop or slide. The exact distance will vary from application to application, but one factor remains. You must be exact in judging the correct distance or your kick will not attain its maximum effectiveness.

4. Execute your kick.

Did you notice anything wrong or improper in this series of photographs? Take another look. See them now?

Notice how I have misjudged the distance between Ron and I when executing the Hopping/Sliding Backward Side Kick. My kicking leg, which is fully extended in photograph number four, actually struck Ron at approximately 95% of full extension, rather than at 75% of full extension where my kick would have been much more effective. In this case, hopping or sliding too far backward generally causes those mistakes. However, you must remember that immediately after you initially hop/slide backwards, you will want to change direction and hop/slide forward slightly as you deliver your kick.

Additionally, if you look at photograph number three; you can see that Ron's punch is fully extended and I am still in the "Coil" position. In this particular instance, this is fully acceptable, and actually preferred as it opens up the armpit area for my kick. Kicking too soon is this situation generally leads to you kicking your opponent's elbow, not the ribs in the armpit area.

Always remember, that the martial arts are 90% mental and 10% physical. Now keeping that in mind, realize that most individuals practice the physical aspect 90% of the time, and the mental aspect 10% of the time, if at all. How do you practice?

Jumping Side Kick:

1. You and your opponent are facing each other in a Closed Position.

2. As your opponent starts to step forward to deliver a punch, you jump straight up into the air and bring your kicking leg up into the "Coil" position.

3. While you are jumping up into the air, bring your kicking leg knee up into the coil position. Ideally, you will strike your opponent at the peak of your jump and at 75% of full-extension. However, most individuals seem to strike their opponent when their non-kicking foot is already back down on the ground. This is not correct.

4. Even though you may be proficient in kicking while one foot remains on the ground, that does not mean that you will automatically transfer that skill over to the execution of aerial kicks. Remember, aerial kicking is an art form unto itself and needs to be practiced only after you have become proficient at executing your primary kicks.

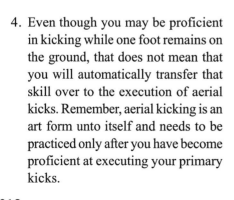

Did you notice anything wrong or improper in this series of photographs? Take another look. See them now?

In photograph number three; it is painfully obvious that I am too far away from Ron in order to effectively kick him. You can see the results of this in photograph number four where my kick is at 100% of full extension and still is about 18 inches short of hitting the target. Not to mention that I have actually kicked over Ron's head instead of through it.

As you look at the entire series of photographs, you can see that the distance between Ron and I is perfect in photographs number one and two. However, if you look a little more closely at photograph number three, you can see that Ron has actually moved backwards away from my kick, rather than just standing there and getting hit. You had better realize now that your opponent is not going to just stand there and let you hit him. He is going to be trying to avoid your attack, while attempting to launch a successful attack of his own. There is a lot more to fighting than just punching and kicking!

Now let's take a look at photograph number four; as I mentioned in the first paragraph, I have not only fallen short of delivering my kick, but I also kicked over my opponent's head. Two very common mistakes that are made when executing almost any type of aerial kick. Were both of these mistakes made by me? No, falling short of the target was not a mistake on my part as my opponent moved backwards after I had initially jumped up in the air. Although you could argue that I might have somehow telegraphed my kick in advance, and that is why Ron knew it was coming and was able to move out of the way.

However, kicking over Ron's head is definitely a mistake that I made and although that mistake is quite common, it is inexcusable. It doesn't matter whether or not you are executing a ground based kick or an aerial kick, you should still be accurately kicking your intended target every time. It is a common misconception that you have to kick high when executing an aerial kick. This is one of the great "urban legends" in martial arts. I have personally used several different aerial kicks in actual self-defense situations, and only two of them were high section kicks. The rest were midsection kicks. And yes, the two high section kicks did connect with my opponents at the time. One ended the fight, while the other left me with numerous openings that I did exploit to my advantage.

Awards & Accomplishments

This is a picture of the first world record certificate that I received from the Guinness Book of World Records for performing 10,502 High Kicks in 5 hours and 30 minutes on September 27, 1986 in Butte, Montana USA.

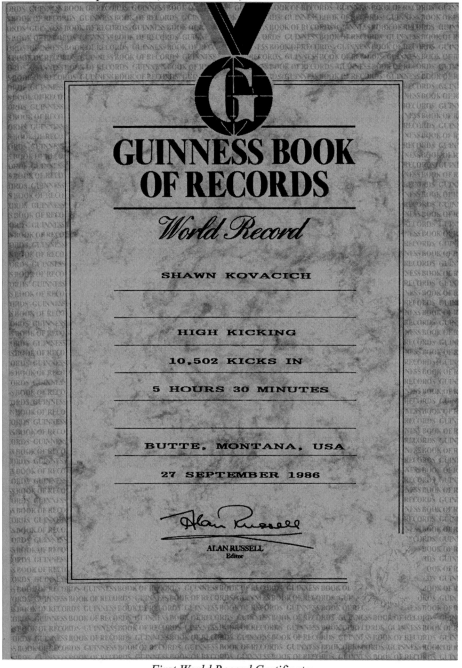

First World Record Certificate

This is a picture of the second world record certificate that I received from the Guinness Book of World Records for performing 11,000 High Kicks in 5 hours 18 minutes and 43 seconds on January 21, 1989 in Anaconda, Montana USA.

WORLD RECORD

GUINNESS BOOK OF RECORDS

THIS IS TO CERTIFY THAT

SHAWN KOVACICH

PERFORMED 11,000 HIGH KICKS

IN 5 HR 18 MIN 43 SEC

AT HARDEE'S RESTAURANT

IN ANACONDA, MONTANA

ON 21 JANUARY 1989

DONALD McFARLAN   NORRIS McWHIRTER

THIS CERTIFICATE DOES NOT NECESSARILY DENOTE AN ENTRY INTO THE GUINNESS BOOK OF RECORDS

Second World Record Certificate

215

This is a picture of the actual letter that I received from The Guinness Book of World Records officially recognizing my second world record for performing 11,000 High Kicks in 5 hours 18 minutes and 43 seconds on January 21, 1989 in Anaconda, Montana USA.

GUINNESS BOOK OF RECORDS

Mr S Kovacich   17 March 1989
211B Main
Anaconda
MT 59711
USA

Dear Mr Kovacich

Thank you for sending us the two signed statements as
requested in our letter of 21 February.

We are now in a position to recognise your achievement as a
new record, and unless we receive details of a better claim
before we go to press, your record will be included in the
1990 book. As mentioned in our letter, however, it is a
category which will be dropped after next year's book.

Enclosed is a certificate in recognition of your record -
congratulations.

Yours sincerely

Nicholas Heath-Brown

Nicholas Heath-Brown
Deputy Editor

33 London Road, Enfield, Middlesex EN2 6DJ. England. Tel: 01-367 4567 Telex: 23573 GBR LDN Fax: 01 367 5912
Guinness Publishing Ltd, Registered Office: 39 Portman Square, London, W1H 9HB. Registered: London 2079632

The above photograph was taken of me circling one of my opponents during a match at the prestigious U.S. Shidokan Open, which is held annually in Chicago, Illinois.

The above photograph was taken of me performing a Side Kick against one of my opponents during a match at the prestigious Sabaki Challenge, which is held annually in Denver, Colorado.

Coming Soon

Achieving Kicking Excellence;™ Applications In Combat: Series

---

Preview of Series:

This ten volume series of books will go into intricate detail on the **Who, What, Where, When, Why, and How** of using each of the ten primary kicks (and their main variations) in a self-defense or combat situation.

This series of books will not teach you **How** to kick, as this has already been covered in volumes one thru ten in the Achieving Kicking Excellence™ series. Instead, it will teach you **How** to apply those kicks in a given situation.

This series of books will cover various contributing factors (from an attackers point of view) such as:

Environment	Conditioning	Avoidance
Time-of-day	Flexibility	Prevention
Clothing	Mind Set	Protecting Others
Shoes	Physiological Conditions	Danger Levels
Witnesses	Weapons	Response Levels
Laws	Awareness	and much, much more!

If you learn how to effectively attack your opponent with kicks, you will be better prepared to use that knowledge to your advantage when your opponent is using those very same kicks against you.

This series of books is scheduled to be released in 2007.

Coming Soon

Achieving Kicking Excellence;[TM]
Defending Against Kicks:
Series

Preview of Series:

This ten volume series of books will go into intricate detail on the **Who, What, Where, When, Why, and How** of defending yourself against each of the ten primary kicks (and their main variations) in a self-defense or combat situation.

This series of books will not teach you **How** to kick, as this has already been covered in volumes one thru ten in the Achieving Kicking Excellence[TM] series. Instead, it will teach you **How** to defend against those kicks in a given situation.

This series of books will cover various contributing factors (from a defenders point of view) such as:

Environment	Conditioning	Avoidance
Time-of-day	Flexibility	Prevention
Clothing	Mind Set	Protecting Others
Shoes	Physiological Conditions	Danger Levels
Witnesses	Weapons	Response Levels
Laws	Awareness	and much, much more!

If you learn how to effectively defend yourself against a kicking attack, you will be better prepared to use that knowledge to your advantage when you are using those kicks against an opponent.

This series of books is scheduled to be released in 2007.

Recommended Reading

Basic Anatomy of the Side Kick

1. Rasch, Philip J. Ph.D. & Burke, Roger K. Ph.D., Kinesiology and Applied Anatomy, (Lea & Febiger, Philadelphia, Pennsylvania, 1978)

2. Gray, Henry F.R.S., Gray's Anatomy, (Running Press, Philadelphia, Pennsylvania, 1974)

Warm Up and Stretching

1. Anderson, Bob, Stretching, (Shelter Publications, Inc., Bolinas, California, 1980)

Basic Principles of Kicking Movement

1. Fixx, James E., Maximum Sports Performance, (Random House, Inc., New York and Toronto, 1985)

2. Loehr, James E., Ed.D., Mental Toughness Training for Sports, (Stephen Greene Press, Inc., 1986)

3. Mashiro, N., Ph.D., Black Medicine: The Dark Art of Death, (Paladin Press, Boulder, Colorado, 1978)

4. Brancazio, Peter J., Sport Science, (Touchstone/Simon & Schuster, Inc., New York, New York, 1985)

5. Adams, Brian, Deadly Karate Blows: The Medical Implications, (Unique Publications, Burbank, California, 1985)

6. Hibbard, Jack, Karate Breaking Techniques: with Practical Applications, (Charles E. Tuttle Company, Inc., Tokyo, Japan, 1981)

Training and Practice Methods

1. Urquidez, Benny "The Jet", Training and Fighting Skills, (Unique Publications, Inc., Burbank, California, 1981)

2. Derse, Ed, Explosive Power-Plyometrics for Bodybuilders, Martial Artists & other Athletes, (Health for Life, Los Angeles, California, 1993)

3. Secrets of Advanced Body Builders, (Health For Life, Los Angeles, California, 1985)

4. Simon, Ilene Caryn, Mind Gains, (Health For Life, Los Angeles, California, 1995)

5. Robinson, Jerry & Carrino, Frank, Max 02 The Complete Guide To Synergistic Aerobic Training, (Health For Life, Los Angeles, California, 1993)

6. The Human Fuel Handbook, (Health For Life, Los Angeles, California, 1988)

Martial Arts & Self-Defense

1. Burke, Dennis R. M.D., Treating Martial Arts Injuries, (Ohara Publications, Inc., Burbank, California, 1981)

2. Echanis, Michael D., Knife Self-Defense for Combat, (Ohara Publications, Inc., Burbank, California, 1977)

3. Echanis, Michael D., Basic Stick Fighting for Combat, (Ohara Publications, Inc., Burbank, California, 1978)

4. Echanis, Michael D., Knife Fighting, Knife Throwing for Combat, (Ohara Publications, Inc., Burbank, California, 1978)

5. Ming, Shi, & Weijia, Siao, Mind Over Matter: Higher Martial Arts, (Frog, Ltd., Berkeley, California, 1994)

6. Canney, J.C. Dr., Health and Fitness in the Martial Arts, (Charles E. Tuttle Co., Inc., Rutland, Vermont, 1988)

7. Siddle, Bruce K., Sharpening the Warrior's Edge, (PPCT Research Publications, Millstadt, Illinois, 1995)

8. Kauz, Herman, The Martial Spirit, (The Overlook Press, Woodstock, New York, 1977)

INDEX

223

tibia, 13-16
tibialis anterior, 16-24
tibialis posterior, 16-24
timing, 35
toes, 13-16, 27, 31-33
training methods, 170-192
training partner, 170, 189-191, 193, 195
trigger, 130
trouble shooting, 193-195
Turning Side Kick, 66-76

U
upper abdomen area, 29
urban legend, 213
USTU, 7

V
variations, 66-169
vastus lateralis, 16-24
vastus medialis, 16-24
visualization, 36
vital point, 28-29, 93, 99, 142, 167
vulnerable, 102, 109
vulnerable point, 28-29, 93, 99, 142, 167, 208

W
wall practice, 172-174, 190, 192
warm-up, 11, 25-26, 66
water training, 190
weak leg, 164
weight, 30
weight lifting belt, 176, 178, 180
weight lifting gloves, 176, 178, 180
wood, 28, 110
wrestling, 201

X
xiphoid process, 29

Notes:

Notes:

Notes:

Notes:

Notes:

Notes:

Notes:

Notes:

Notes:

Notes: